# From Me

# to

# You xxx

*A true love story revealed in letters,*
*written by L R Olszewski from 1965 to 1968*

*edited by M Olszewska*

Grosvenor House
Publishing Limited

This book is published by
Grosvenor House Publishing Ltd
Link House
140 The Broadway, Tolworth, Surrey, KT6 7HT.
www.grosvenorhousepublishing.co.uk

A CIP record for this book
is available from the British Library

ISBN 978-1-80381-414-8

For the other girls he loves.

Adrienne, Natasha and Bronia,
his daughter and granddaughters.

On the last night of the Blackpool Illuminations, in October 1965, a 17-year-old boy met a 17-year-old girl on the dance floor of the Tower Ballroom. Later that evening, after a few drinks, a kiss and a cuddle at the coach station, he said to her, 'Will you write to me?'

She said to him, 'Will you write back?'

He did!

October 1965

Dear M,

Thanks very much for your very nice letter. During a break I had between eating my dinner and doing prefect duties at school, I dashed home on my high-powered motorcycle just to see if your letter had arrived and, much to my delight, it had. I wasn't sure if you would actually write as you said but I'm so glad you did.

The club you go to seems to be a fab place. There are a few jazz clubs here in Blackpool but I've never been to any of them. I tend to go to the Tower or sometimes the Mecca.

Tonight is the annual swimming gala, which is held jointly with the local girls' grammar school. I don't think I'll bother going so I'll watch **Panorama** or something instead.

On Sunday I did some school work in the morning and in the afternoon I went for a ride on my motorbike to Bleasdale Fells. I really like the rugged scenery and the winding roads make a great bike ride.

From your letter, it sounds as if you have a longer half term holiday than us, a whole week. We just have four days. It's a bit longer than usual but not long enough!

1

I have a sneaking suspicion that this letter is becoming rather boring for you so if it is please accept my most humble apologies. While I'm at it, I must apologise for my scrawl. Your writing, by the way, I thought was very neat.

After you left on Saturday night I thought a lot about you and wished we had met the week before because then we could have been together on Saturday for a second time.

I just watched **Stramash!** on the old idiot box. It's a bit old-fashioned but all in all not too bad. The Three Bells were on in the Ocean Room last Christmas Eve. They were better then because they did loads of Crystals and Ronettes songs.

I won't indulge in the rather juvenile pastime of spattering the envelope with such gems as S.A.M. or B.U.R.M.A., etc., so I'll finish with loads of love.

With loads of love, L xxx

P.S. I've thought about you a lot so could you possibly send me a photo of you so I can keep it under my pillow or somewhere then every time I think of you I can look at it and remember you even more.

P.P.S. That was a bit 'sloppy', but I meant every word of it.

Lots of love, L xxxxx

October 1965

Dear M,

Thanks very much for your second letter. I must confess, however, that I wasn't sure what 'platonic' meant. **The New English Dictionary John Bull Edition** gives it as 'pure spiritual affection between the sexes' (whatever that means).

I'm writing this letter in bed so please excuse the writing. S.A.M. is rather a feeble expression standing for 'Sex at Midnight' and B.U.R.M.A. is 'Be Undressed Ready My Angel'. Doesn't sound very platonic, does it?

I don't have a regular girlfriend and even if I did it would not affect our friendship.

On Wednesday while playing rugby for the school, I received a black eye that's going to last for weeks but I'll survive.

I don't have any regular penfriends, but I do write occasionally to a lad who now lives in Stockport who is going to join the RAF when he finishes school.

From your letters I get the impression that you have rather a prolific pen - like Hal David and Burt Bacharach - that sounds like a Jewish name. Speaking of religion, I'm an atheist myself. How about you?

The farthest 'abroad' I've been is Leuchars, in Scotland, for a week two years ago. It was an ATC

3

summer camp. This year my holiday was a day flight to the Isle of Man to watch the Manx Grand Prix races.

At the end of your letter you mentioned seeing me again. I want to see you again naturally but it's a bit difficult cos I have to play rugby every Saturday afternoon. But I would be able to come on Sunday, or perhaps arrive Saturday evening and go back Sunday if I could find somewhere to stay. If I don't have too much to drink, I can always come on my machine then I would be able to leave later as buses take hours. Anyway, I'll definitely come and see you during the Christmas vacation.

I'm running out of things to say so I'll sign off now,

Lots of love,

L xxxxx

P.S. I haven't got a recent picture of myself but I'll get one for you.

P.P.S. still thinking of you. L x

October 1965

Dear M,

Thank you very much for your rather revealing letter. When it arrived I was on the point of deciding whether to do some school work or nothing at all so I decided to write this letter to you.

I agree with most things you said but I don't think there is any need for any kind of faith or religion in this day and age, but I shall see if *Heaven and Hell* is in the town library.

I think that the punishments for a lot of serious crimes are not severe enough i.e., more hanging. I also think that motoring crimes such as dangerous or drunken driving, from which severe injury or even death results, need more severe penalties.

I think the bomb should be kept as a deterrent, but I don't have any strong views on segregation as I don't really understand it. I know the British have taken great advantage through slave-trading and colonialism, but it doesn't really affect my conscience.

I have nothing against sex before marriage and if I marry I am not particularly interested whether the girl is a virgin or not, either by myself or anyone else, although my parents would probably not approve. In any case, my private life and how I behave depends on my own standards and not theirs. Some people may think this is a rather harsh attitude to parents considering all the sacrifices they make for us especially when we are young, but I believe in what I think to be true and there's nothing wrong with this, is there? (I hope that makes proper sense).

I am not very interested in politics but if I could vote I would probably vote Liberal. I think that the Tories are weak and vague in their actions and opinions, especially since Ted Heath took over. I thought he was at his 'peak' at the common market fiasco. He's all right in power but in opposition he doesn't seem to be quite sure how to go about it.

I must say I am in complete agreement with you about the queen. What need is there for a monarchy today? - none whatsoever in my opinion. I know it's good for tourism etc., but it costs the public lots of money to support all the minor royals and their offspring.

I'm not all that keen on sport but I do like rugby because it's a way of letting off steam and releasing my pent-up emotions (to use a rather overused cliché). I am always getting into fights and have been threatened with being sent off on a number of occasions for being aggressive. Sometimes I have been injured and this year I have been knocked out a couple of times. Last year I broke my collarbone twice! I like tennis when you can play it properly. It's a fast, exciting game but when you start it's a bit feeble because you can neither serve properly nor have any rallies of more than about one hit each.

Last Saturday night I stayed in for the first time for ages. What a drag it was! I stayed in so I would have some money to buy my ma a birthday present. I watched television all night. That's bad enough but Saturday night it's worse than...? (Can't think of a word). The only thing worth watching is BBC3 and **On the Braden Beat**. I like these satire sort of programmes, especially with Peter Cook and Dudley Moore. Did you see DM in **Love Story** on Monday night? It was rather a disappointment. If he is considering being an actor I would have thought he would have picked a stronger and more interesting play.

Can't think of anything else.

Lots of love, L xxx

P.S. Hope this wasn't too long or boring but I just couldn't help it. My pen just kept on uncontrollably writing.

P.P.S. Please excuse my SPG - English was never one of my strong points.

Again - lots of love, L.

November 1965

Dear M,

Thanks very much for your letter.

Last Friday there was a joint debate with the girls' grammar school.

The motion should interest you: 'Marriage is obsolete'. The first girl to speak opened with this leading question: 'Will all bastards please stand up?' Needless to say, one fool from our school stood up. The motion was defeated by 89 to 13.

Having looked at myself in the mirror for a few minutes, I will attempt to describe myself; height five-feet-eight, weight eleven and a half stones, hair dark brown and curly, and eyes greyish. I have very long eyelashes which seem to be the envy of most females of my acquaintance and that's about it. I will try to send a photo at some point.

I watched **Miss World** on Friday. I thought Miss Finland was the best but I 'fancied' Miss Austria the most. Of the others I thought Miss Ireland was the most natural-looking. Miss UK and USA were all smiles and typical beauty contestants. I know you don't really like it and compare it to a cattle market but millions of people watch it.

Last Saturday I stayed in for a change and watched **BB3**. Dennis Norton is good and John Bird does a fantastic impression of Harold Wilson and an even better one of Joshua Nkomo over which there was all that fuss.

I like rugged scenery especially coasts, like east Scotland around Edinburgh. I like the Trough of Bowland and the moors like Ilkley. I prefer dramatic scenery to flat and boring places. I'm not keen on camping or hiking but I like biking. I am against hitchhiking and I certainly would not give any lifts to anyone if I had a car. It's a bit early to say what's happening at Christmas or New Year. Pete will be happy that you and Hilary might even end up here.

I'll finish now.

Lots of love, L xxxxx

November 1965

Dear M,

I'm sorry this letter has taken so long to arrive but I've been absolutely inundated with school work and have not had time to write a proper letter.

I don't read much but have phases when I read about three books a week for a month or two and then I don't read anything for months. After my first A-levels, when I had plenty of time on my hands, I read the Keith Waterhouse books - **Billy Liar, There is a Happy Land** and **Jubb**. I enjoyed **Billy Liar** the most but I thought **There is a Happy Land** was more true to life. He seemed to be able to capture most accurately young children's way of thought, actions and emotions. Although I've never read any Jean Paul Sartre or Zola I did see one of Sartre's plays on the goggle box. I think it was called **The Room**. The room was supposed to represent hell and it showed the way three different people (two women and one man) react to it. I think the three people were all sinners or something. Anyway, I thought it was one of the best plays that has been on TV.

I do not think much of religion and have quite a low opinion of the Catholic Church. If I had to sum it up, I would call it 'Instant Forgiveness'. It seems to me that if you are a Catholic you can sin all week at will then as long as you confess on Sunday it's all right. I have quite a low opinion of most of the other religions too. I can't see why the Catholic Church still hold out against contraception the way they do. To me it's obvious that it will be accepted in time so why wait when approving it now can save so much suffering and king-size families, etc.? I feel that having sex is the complete way of showing love and affection and is not just an act for producing a child, which the Catholic Church seems to think.

I don't have much time for horoscopes. Most of their predictions are rash generalisations although sometimes, I must admit, that the type of person you are can coincide with what you are told in **Old Moore's Almanac**, etc. I would be very interested to hear what it says about you and what you really think you are.

I'm against comprehensive education because I don't think it is any better than the present system. I suppose both systems have their DIS- and AD-vantages. I'm probably subconsciously prejudiced because I go to a grammar school myself.

I've been filling in my UCCA form at last and my choices are, in this order: Liverpool, Birmingham, Nottingham, Swansea, Salford CAT and Brunel.

I hope you haven't been too bored by my ramblings.

Lots of love, L xxx

P.S. *Good luck at Edgehill.*

P.P.S. *Excuse me for showing my ignorance but what sort of college is Edgehill?*
   *Again, lots of love, L xxxx*

November 1965

Dear M,

I hope to do metallurgy at university, if I get there, that is. I would have preferred to do physics or some sort of engineering but my maths isn't up to much. If I don't get in I'll probably join the civil service.

Someone told me that Edgehill is a hard place to get into so if you are accepted it will be no mean achievement.

Earlier in the week, we had the annual memorial lecture. It's a lecture in memory of the old boys who died in the wars. This year we got a chap from Keele University who spoke on 'Soldiers and Politics in the Modern World'. It was quite interesting but he kept on repeating himself. Most people will only remember that he said that in Somalia there are 47 ways of saying 'a camel' because they are so common. In Latin America, there are loads of ways of saying 'revolution' for the same reason.

I always go to the Remembrance Service at the cenotaph in Blackpool. It makes me sad, especially the words, that end, 'With the setting of the sun, and in the morning we shall remember them' and one of the tunes they always play. I think it is **Jupiter** from **The Planet Suite**. I like to see the old soldiers from the Great War proudly wearing all their medals then limping and hobbling in the parade after the service.

What sort of music do you prefer? I like pop but I can listen to classical music. I prefer the slow, sad type not the loud '1812' type. I like some folk music and some Bob Dylan. I used to have loads of Buddy Holly records when I was younger but I sold them. I like Booker T and the MGs and some old Elvis stuff from the **Jailhouse Rock** and **King Creole** era.

Last night at the film society we had **On the Waterfront** with Marlon Brando. Sometimes in his films it's really hard to tell what he's talking about, and this was no exception. I think it was a bit boring with not much action. We sometimes used to get French or Italian comedies with subtitles but those days are over, thank God. The next film is **Some like it Hot** - no description necessary!

None of your views shock or disgust me. In fact, it takes a lot more to shock me. (I think you know what I'm getting at).

Still thinking of you. Love, L xxxxx

November 1965

Dear M,

It hasn't snowed here but it sleets every day and it's really cold.

On Wednesday we went to Keighley to play rugby (lost 3-0) and were within four or five miles of your place but I didn't notice any snow anywhere.

I've just come in out of the cold after queuing up for ages to get some bread because of this stupid bread strike. According to the papers, people have been fighting in bread queues in London. What would Marie Antoinette have said? Let them eat cake (or biscuits)!

I went to the pictures for the second time in a week. I went to see **Hush Hush Sweet Charlotte**. From the reviews I had read I expected it to be well worth seeing but it wasn't. Granted there were some blood-curdling scenes and excellent acting but it just dragged on for half an hour too long. If the story had been used for one of the Hitchcock's hour-long TV programmes it would have been a lot better. The other film I saw was **Moll Flanders**. It was quite good but I only really went cos Kim Novak was in it. I think she's got the most sexy eyes I've ever seen. Anyway, I've gone off her a bit because she's married.

I took Thursday off school this week. I started reading all the essays in my old English books. They were a scream. I didn't intend them to be funny at the time. They're full of unrelated paragraphs and waffle to fill up the required four pages or six hundred words or whatever it was we had to write.

The name of my school is just plain Blackpool Grammar School. The one you were thinking of was King Edward VII in Lytham.

Now I'm not too sure I want to go to college. It's not the moving or making new friends but having to study all the time. I heard from a friend who went to Southampton and he says it's all go with no time for social activities. Another thing is trying to survive on a grant. I would probably overspend early on and be in debt at the end.

Lots of love, L xxxxx

P.S. Yesterday the temperature was below freezing and our school dinner was cold salad! I hope it warms up as on Saturday I'll have to run around half-naked playing rugby. Brrrr.

Again, lots of love, L xxxxx

December 1965

Dear M,

The dreaded snow caught up with us on Sunday so there was a thick covering but unfortunately not enough to prevent me from travelling to school on Monday. By Tuesday most of it had gone.

Last weekend a group of us went to the Mecca for a discotheque. It was a bit of a failure as everybody was doing mod dances à la **Ready Steady Go!** which none of us could do. The records played consisted of the usual American stuff like **Let's hang on**, **Run Baby Run**, **Midnight Hour** ad infinitum and ad nauseum. A sore point was the Mecca prices for drinks. A mere Coca Cola can cost two shillings a time. They must make a fair profit as they probably only cost them sixpence.

At our school absences must be verified by a doctor's or parent's note. If I feel like a day off I can usually talk my mum into writing me a note but my dad doesn't know. We sometimes 'forge' notes for mates who just want some time off. Last summer, after A-levels, we were left to our own devices so after morning registration we escaped until dinner time, had our school dinner, did afternoon registration and then scarpered.

I've not heard from any universities yet. I must admit I'm terrified of interviews. Apparently some interview you about things which lie outside the A-level syllabuses which they expect you to have read. I don't do any of this 'expected work', just what's set for homework. That's all I do and no more. It's a bit of a shop steward approach I suppose.

I will definitely vote when I can. I'd probably vote Liberal for no reason except I don't think much of the others. No offence to you but I think some women waste their vote by thinking, 'Hmm he looks nice so I'll vote for him.'

You said that you had been abroad, didn't you? I haven't but I hope to in the future. Did anything exciting happen while you were in Paris? (The mad city where only the river is Seine) I suppose you went to the Eiffel Tower and Notre Dame. I'd like to go there sometime.

School is now worse than having a tombstone tied around my neck. Having done it all before, most lessons seem even more boring than last year. The one advantage is I've done practically all the same homework already so I can just copy it out again. It won't do me much good but it saves time.

On **University Challenge** they've just asked where the word 'supercalifragilisticexpialidocious' was first coined. No need to ask you, is there? I'll bet you know the words of every song in that film plus the cost of every lolly and ice cream.

Still thinking of you.

Love, L xxxxx

December 1965

Dear M,

I've just had to push my motorbike home in weather which would rival that in India during the monsoon season. I'm so disheartened that I can't be bothered to go to the school play tonight. This year it's **A Man for All Seasons** by Bolt. It's about Thomas More and Henry VIII and the divorce of one of his wives. It's not really my sort of thing.

My A-level subjects are maths, chemistry and physics. I was in the express form so I took them a year early. This year I'm supposedly trying to improve my grades. My only minority subjects are general studies for the general paper, which I failed last year. I used to do three periods of cultural French but it became optional so I packed it in. I do one period of RI in which we have long discussions about the need for religion and the existence of God. I used to do Russian, which I liked, probably because the master had absolutely no control over us so we talked and threw paper aeroplanes around the room.

I've just read a Jean Paul Sartre novel called **The Age of Reason**. It's about a chap whose mistress gets pregnant after seven years (not surprisingly) and wants an abortion but the chap is short of money.

I thought it was a bit too long drawn out. I didn't like the way he describes people's feelings as colours and the way he puts down their thoughts. Have you read it? I then started **No Highway** by Neville Shute. It wasn't until about page 90 before I realised I'd read it previously.

This week I have been on bus queue duty, which means, at the end of school, stopping the massed charge of howling little brats storming the buses and squashing the unsuspecting bus conductors. It's an impossible task even if all the prefects actually turn up for it.

Do you like **Keep on Running** by the Spencer Davies Group? Stevie Winwood, the singer, is the same age as us, but his voice sounds much older. I also like **Rescue me** by Fontella Bass.

I haven't much homework this weekend so I can devote most of my time to routine maintenance on my bike to find out what the heck is up with the thing.

Do you want me to send you a Christmas card? I don't usually send them but I will if you send me one.

That's all for now.

Love, L xxxx

P.S. How do you know that French firemen are sexier than ours?

December 1965

Dear M,

Thanks for your letter.

Liverpool have contacted me and they say they'll have me if I get a D for chemistry and maths (got Es last year) so I suppose I'll be able to get in if I pass the Use of English exam. Have you heard from anywhere yet?

At the moment it's a bit of a drag seeing all the holiday advertisements in the papers when I know full well I shan't be able to go on any. This year my parents are going to Southern Ireland (without me - thank God) so when they are away I'll have a continuous six-day party, even if I am supposed to be at school.

I don't believe in ghosts but there are several seemingly unanswered questions like how do the Dervishes stick swords in each other without dying? How can hypnotised people be made to float, etc.? Sometimes I get the feeling that I have been to a place before, or have done something before. It's quite an eerie feeling isn't it? Most of these experiences have been at school of all places.

Our headmaster seems to be having a 'get tough' policy at the moment by really enforcing school rules. The entire school could be thrown into detention during this great purge. There must be no smoking, no long hair, no pointed-toed shoes, ties must be correctly tied and everyone must wear ankle-length, blue, Gestapo-style raincoats. They only abolished compulsory wearing of caps for sixth-formers a couple of years ago

I see that Somerset Maugham has passed away. Have you ever read any of his books? If you have, tell me a title and we can compare notes on it. Lately I have read lots of books on atomic war where everyone either goes insane or dies off. Perhaps I have an inborn, hidden until now, infatuation with nuclear disasters and annihilation. You mentioned CND in one of your letters. You're not in it are you? I'm all for keeping the bomb and I don't think Cannon Collins, and people who try to board Polaris submarines have a cat in hell's chance of achieving anything. I don't approve of clergymen giving out messages to politicians about how to direct their policies. They should stop sticking their oars in.

Have you ever fancied being an actor? The life of an actor quite appeals to me so long as I wouldn't be acting the same part in a play that has a ten year run. I would fancy acting in films but I haven't got enough courage for such a career so it comes under the category of 'pipe dreams'.

Coming back to summer again, I'm going to apply for a summer job as a conductor on the trams or buses. It's hard work but the pay is quite good. They say money can't buy happiness but it goes a long way to getting it, doesn't it?

Still thinking of you.

Lots of love, L xxxxx

December 1965

Dear M,

Your holiday in France seemed to be very enjoyable.
I haven't been abroad but I'd like to. I did go to
London to see an air show at Biggin Hill. Have you
ever been on the Underground? If you did, did you
feel scared? I did. The trains seem to hurtle through
the tunnels at the speed of light swaying from side to
side and when they take a bend it feels as if they are
on the verge of leaving the track. We twice got
on a tube going in the wrong direction. Just how
people find their way around the Underground
I don't know.

Apart from London, the farthest from home I've
been is Leuchars in Scotland, near St Andrews. It
was an Air Training Corps summer camp. When one
goes to one's first summer camp, one is initiated
according to ancient custom. They have 'blacking',
'tooth-pasting' and plain ducking. There has to be a
reason for being initiated such as telling an NCO
where to go when he tells you, you are on ablution
duty. If they can't find a similar reason they make
one up, such as being accused of being a communist
for wearing a red jumper. The 'trial' then takes
place and you are guilty until proved innocent.

Inevitably, you are found guilty and sentenced. 'Blacking' involves a certain male organ being smeared in shoe polish with a shoe brush. 'Tooth-pasting' is similar and ducking speaks for itself. 'Tooth-pasting' is the worst because it really stings. The best way of removing either polish or toothpaste is by 'washing' it in hair cream. How on earth that was discovered I don't know.

Once I had been made a corporal and had some responsibility to teach little brats about the fundamentals of the internal combustion engine or aerodynamics, I decided to retire. That was over a year ago and I still have the uniform in my wardrobe.

Do you always find Christmas Day an anti-climax after a Christmas Eve night out? I always seem to get up late, eat my Christmas dinner then watch **The African Queen, The Charge of the Light Brigade**, or other such rubbish.

I'm at a loss for words now so I'll sign off.

Lots of love, L xxxxx

January 1966

Dear M,

Please excuse the rather feeble birthday card. It was the only slightly humorous one they had.

In one of your letters you said you quite liked poetry. I can't compose poems very successfully as I get all the iambic pentameter and that all mixed up except in simple things like this -

Verse 1:
    The thing that came from the sea
    Looked like an overgrown flea
    With big mince pies for its eyes
    And clothes pegs for its legs.

Verse 10:
    The thing began to moan
    As it made its way home
    Then it sadly sighed
    And closed its eyes and died.

I wrote that one for a homework a few years ago and I'll spare you verses 2-9. I only got about one and a half out of ten for it which I felt was a little mean.

Here's something more appropriate courtesy of Heman's **Poetical Works**. 'Oh that these lips had language - life hath passed with me but roughly since I saw thee last'. I must have overdone the Newcastle Brown again!

'Oh, if the soul immortal be, is not its love immortal too?' - I can't say that I couldn't get to sleep because of thinking of you. I went out like a light (Newcastle Brown again) but I am thinking of you now.

Lots of love, L xxxx

PS, last but not least:

'As are our hearts, our way is one, and cannot be divided. Strong affection contends with all things and overcometh all things. Will I not live with thee? Will I not cheer thee? Wouldst thou be lonely then? Wouldst thou be sad?'

Again, lots of love, L xxx

*January 1966*

*Dear M,*

*Please excuse the paper. I'm so broke I can barely afford the stamp! I must say I wasn't quite happy about sending that card. Sorry*

*What sort of humour do you like? I like all sorts, particularly the Bob Newhart and Shelly Berman type. I also like Patrick Campbell of course. He's about the most spontaneous liar that ever walked the Emerald Isle. The only British comedian I really like is Frankie Howard. On the radio, I like **Round the Horne** and **Beyond our Ken**.*

*I went to see **What's New Pussycat** last night. I thought it was a scream. I think Peter O'Toole took most of the limelight from Peter Sellars though. I've only seen one Peter Sellars film before, when I was about twelve I think. In it, he played an old watchmaker or something. It wasn't funny and I couldn't make head nor tail of it.*

*I have slept with girls. When you read this letter, I'll bet that last sentence came as a rather abrupt change of topic and seriousness. What do I think about girls? Well it's hard to say really. As a rule they are sensible enough - that sounds a feeble comment but it's all that comes to mind. I must say it's refreshing writing to you because most girls*

I know only seem to want to talk about the top ten or Mick Jagger. In the past I have found it a bit of a drag being with girls of your intelligence but I can get along fine with you. I think it's because I can talk more easily with you - besides, I like you a lot.

Fancy some more poetry?

'Clasp me a little longer on the brink of fate while I can feel thy dear caress. And when this heart hath ceased to beat oh think and let it mitigate thy woe's excess - that thou to me hast been all tenderness'.

NB, disregard the fact that it's about death - it sounds better then.

It's unfortunate for you having your mock exams so early. Ours isn't until 5th March (my birthday). I think I did my first eleven-plus exam on my birthday.

Did you say you might be coming over to Blackpool soon? I hope so.

'Yeah on the scaffold if it needs must be, I will never forsake thee' - Makes a change doesn't it.

Still thinking of you.

Lots of love, L xxxx

*January 1966*

*Dear M,*

*Please excuse my writing. I've been outside all morning trying to get my bike going, so my hands are like blocks of ice. Just before I came in, I made a major breakthrough and it now starts. I was quite depressed about it but feel much better now. You said that going for a walk was always beneficial when you're feeling low. I'll try to remember that next time the thing breaks down.*

*I do like an occasional cigarette but I only smoke when I go out, never at home as my ma and pa don't like me to. Both of them are ex-smokers, so I suppose that's why. If I wanted, I could give up smoking tomorrow. I am one of the best 'tappers' of cigarettes (scrounger to the uninitiated).*

*Do you ever watch **Gideon's Way**? I do. I think I watch it because it brings out the sadist in me. In practically every episode someone gets either clubbed or stabbed to death. I also like to watch **BBC3** and **The Frost Report**. It's surprising really how TV affects your life. When the thing packs up you just sit around wondering what to do. What on earth did people do before it was invented? Listen to the radio, play cards or just go to bed early?*

One of my friends at school operates the projector whenever we get any films. He was telling me that he showed a film about sex education to the second form. He was most disappointed because after an opening shot of a bedroom the film changed over to diagrams with a commentary. Were you ever told the facts of life at school? We weren't. We had a big biology textbook and we did the chapter before and the chapter after the one about sex. I suppose they wanted us to read it for ourselves or perhaps the master was just too embarrassed to tackle it.

I don't do much when I'm on holiday. I usually stay in and listen to the radio in the mornings. In the afternoon I see my friends and talk about motorbikes, play England's most popular sport next to sex, i.e. football, and I sometimes go fishing in the summer.

The next time I see you remember this old Polish proverb: 'Niebezpieczie jest bawic sie ognium'

All my love L xxxxxx

PS Polish into English - It's dangerous to play with fire!

January 1966

Dear M,

We went to see **Cat Balou** on Wednesday. It was quite good. I believe Lee Marvin won some sort of Oscar for his portrayal of Kid Shalee but I didn't think he was particularly deserving of it. He gave a good performance but it wasn't outstanding. Usually when the critics recommend such and such a film they don't usually live up to expectations. Do you find this?

If I were you I wouldn't worry so much about the mocks - please don't think I'm being patronising giving you advice. The only people who think it's of the utmost importance seem to be the head teacher and your own parents. There's loads of time between the mocks and the real thing for any revision. Last year I did a fortnight for the mocks and a week for the exams proper, plus revision in class.

At the moment I am all of a jitter about my interview on Friday. I'm sure to make an absolute mess of it. I was given a mock interview at school yesterday and it didn't go well. I'm going to need all the luck you wished me

Inspiration is now exhausted so...

Lots of love, L xxxxx

PS, I suppose you know what a Liverpudlian replied to the question:

'What would you do if Jesus Christ came to Liverpool tomorrow?'

'I'd play Ian St John at outside right!'

February 1966

Dear M,

Did you get my Valentine's card? It was a toss-up between that one and one with 'stay as sweet as you are' on the cover and a picture of a gorilla staring out at you when you opened it.

This is another letter written in bed and for once I really am ill. I played rugby at Leigh on Saturday (lost 11-13) and I've got a really bad cold and cough. After seeing the town I know why Georgie Fame went to London.

I've never really thought about life in general. I want to have loads of money, doesn't everyone? I'd like to be reasonably happy. Many people think that money can't buy happiness. In my opinion it can. It can make you ninety-nine and nine tenths happy. As long as you have ample money to pay bills, mortgage etc., you have nothing to worry about.

Looking round my bedroom I have discovered that there are 69 articles on the wall. There are such gems as an RAF sick bag, an airline ticket, a poppy, LP sleeves and postcards. The floor is covered in aviation and motorbike magazines and physics and chemistry notes. Do you collect souvenirs?

I've just been listening to Manx radio and have made the astounding discovery that 111 women are seeking employment on the island, and someone lost a handkerchief on Sunday somewhere in Douglas. The Railway A team are just leading the **Examiner** darts league after being beaten 6-3 by the Clarendon. It's all go over there.

In our school library there is a peg board for notices. Just for a laugh we changed 'Library Hours' to 'Library Whores' 2:00-4:00 - very juvenile I know.

Still thinking of you.

All my love, L xxxx

February 1966

Dear M,

It sounds as if you like going round museums and galleries. I'm of the opinion that if you've seen one, you've seen 'em all. The only sections I like are the ones concerning weapons, torture machines, ship models, etc., and the section with prehistoric monsters carefully assembled from thousands of pieces. I have only been to our local art gallery once and even then I was press-ganged into going because a friend of mine had a painting in an exhibition of children's art.

I have no particular favourite style of painting. For a picture to get praise from me it has to produce a favourable reaction because of good brushwork or composition, etc. I can appreciate 'good' art but I am doubtful about the value put on them. No picture is worth thousands just because someone famous painted it. **Grandes Baigneuses**? It's a load of rubbish as are those old religious paintings with fat cherubs floating about the place. I like 'pop art' reproductions such as **Chinese Girl** and **Elephants**. I don't really get Picasso but I do like some abstract paintings composed of many colours and shapes or just black and white geometrical forms. One chap in New York gets a hundred dollars for plain black canvasses and they are selling like hot cakes. Good luck to him while it lasts. I can draw almost anything except people's faces but I'm not much good at painting.

The other week our head boy (a bit of a twit really) sent to the girls' grammar school a large, coloured picture of a rather buxom nude female, with one slight modification - a pencil drawn and appropriately coloured girls' school tie. We are eagerly awaiting what they send us in return.

Still thinking of you.

Love, L xxxxx

March 1966

Thanks for the birthday card. It made me laugh.

The mock exams are just starting. I tried to learn all my physics on Sunday with limited success. At least you seem to have confidence in me.

Next Friday I have to go to London for an interview at Brunel College, Acton. If I have time, I will probably try to visit my long-lost cousin who lives near London Airport.

I hope you will soon be coming over to Blackpool then I will be able to see you after all this time. If it's possible I will try my utmost (what a funny word!) to come and see you during the Easter holidays. At the moment I can see nothing which can prevent me.

I think my parents are going away for a week in May so you could come and stay here for a few days if you like.

I have just applied to the corporation for a job during the summer holidays. It's dishing out deck chairs. The work isn't hard but if there is a sudden downpour in the middle of an otherwise fine, sunny day, all the visitors are prone to abandoning their chairs and finding shelter which means that you have to retrieve them all on your own. If it's raining when you start in the morning it means you will be sent off to Stanley Park to prune the roses or some other gardening job.

My conscience is telling me to get on with some revision.

Still thinking of you, L xxxxxxxxxxxx (I mean to collect these)

March 1966

Dear M,

We too are having a mock election at school. The voting is limited to fifth- and sixth-formers. There are even special ballot papers being printed. All the major parties are represented plus 'The National Teenage Party'. The best parts of the campaign for the MP for our 'constituency' are the political meetings where we can heckle away to our hearts' content.

This morning we had a hair check at school. They are so particular nowadays that they sometimes use a ruler to measure the length of hair and anyone found with sideboards of more than half an inch has to have them shortened by the following day.

We have the school photograph tomorrow. It's a gargantuan thing about a yard long and nine inches high. The chap who takes it dresses and acts like Charlie Chaplin. It's a good laugh and we usually miss half a morning's lessons.

The film at the last film society meeting was **Some Like it Hot** with Marilyn Monroe which, needless to say, went down very well with the male members of the audience. There was some rowdiness during the film resulting in a lecture about setting a good example, etc., etc.

I read **Peyton Place** at weekend. It was a load of rubbish as was **Return to Peyton Place**. At the moment I'm halfway through **Honest to God** but I'm finding it rather hard going.

I don't reckon much to either opera or ballet. Operas tend not to be in English so you can't tell what they're singing about and ballet just seems like lots of fancy jumping around the stage. Apart from pantomimes when I was younger, I have been to the theatre to see a serious play. Billie Whitelaw was in it and it was about Catholics and Protestants in Liverpool. It was in those days of old when the Beatles were undiscovered so no one could understand a genuine Liverpool accent. It was a bit of a waste of time really.

I suppose you heard what happened when a woman in a topless dress went to church? The vicar had a stroke!

Love, Les xxxx


P.S. If you want I can come over on the bus and see you during the Easter holidays.

March 1966

Dear M,

So far this Easter has been a waste of time really. The only time I went out was to the Tower, of course. We came across someone who knows you. I think she was called Linda. She was short and plump and was a bit rowdy. I think she said she was a comptometer operator.

I'm in the middle of my dinner and I'm on the point of attacking a rather sickly-looking meringue so please excuse any fingerprints on the paper.

My bike is still off the road so I am more or less confined to barracks so it's a good job there's some racing to watch this afternoon. I'll wait till the rain stops then have a go at trying to fix it.

I just managed to scrape a grade 3 pass in the Use of English exam so I'll probably be able to get into Liverpool. How did you get on?

I've just been reading **The Persuasion Industry**. It's a book about advertising and it's really interesting. I never realised there was so much research and psychology which had to be done before the advertising campaign was actually started. It said that the advertising campaign for Strand cigarettes was correct in every detail, i.e. presentation, catchphrase, etc., etc., but it just didn't sell the cigarettes. The reason still baffles both the industry and the psychologists.

I see that you have been taking your dog for 'walkies'. We used to have a dog which was a bull mastiff. It used to give me rides round the garden. We sold it a couple of years ago. I believe he was spending his later years at a stud farm (he had a pedigree as long as your arm) - what a way to go! I like dogs but not really little lap dogs and I'm not keen on poodles with funny haircuts.

I'd like to come and see you over Easter if that's OK. I can come on the bus so let me know when.

Still thinking of you.

All my love, L xxxxxx

*April 1966*

*Dear M,*

*How are you? I'm hardly aware of anything after a weekend of ultra-concentrated revision.*

*I couldn't get hold of **The Perfumed Garden** but I have read **The Karma Sutra**. I found it a bit boring after a while. **Fanny Hill** had the same effect on me but nevertheless interesting in parts. I pity the chaps who only have small lingams who feel that they are a bit inferior and hang on weights to try to make it elephant-sized. If I only had a small lingam I would search around for a female in a similar position and not bother about any further extension.*

*The Arts Ball wasn't too bad. Usually I find these late dances a bit of a drag towards the end but I always go at the beginning in case I miss anything.*

*The idea of being a professional artist quite appeals to me. If it returned a fair amount of cash I wouldn't mind living in Paris passing my time away just painting the Seine or Notre Dame.*

*I believe there aren't any pubs in France instead practically every café has a bar. I also understand that you don't have to be 18 to buy alcohol and that for around seven bob you can get the equivalent of a* quadruple vodka and lime that is actually vodka and lime and not vice versa. Is it true that contraceptives are illegal in France? Not sure.

Have you heard from any universities? I got an unconditional from the college I went to in London but I rejected it. I also got the forms necessary for obtaining a grant. I can hardly understand them let alone fill the things in. As I see it, I think you get more if you're married so if we end up at the same place we can always get married to get some extra cash.

Can't think of anything else.

All my love, L xxxx

P.S. When you do Latin do you still have sentences like, 'Brutus, having exhorted his men to fight with the utmost pugnacity and valour against the innumerable numbers of the insidious enemy, went home and had his tea'?

P.P.S. Feeling happy at the moment so here's a joke - girl goes hitchhiking on continent and gets back pregnant - tells her ma who says, 'Are you sure? Have you had a check-up?' - Reply, 'No it was a Hungarian.'

Loads of love, L

xxxx

*April 1966*

*Dear M,*

*I'm sorry you're not too well but you can't really be thinking of signing the pledge. I just had to write to you as I need a welcome break. I've been doing chemistry problems at the rate of three an hour and there are still six to go.*

*My 'rash' is just starting to fade. I'll have to make a better job of yours next time we meet. Having seen you three times lately, I'm quite sad as we probably won't meet again for a while. It's a pity we have to live so far apart as it makes face-to-face communication difficult.*

*Did you see The Loving Spoonfuls on TV last night? Don't you think **Daydream** is a really fab record? I also like **Dedicated Follower of Fashion** by the Kinks and **You Don't Have to Say you Love me** by Busty Dusty.*

*The sun is shining today. It would have been great on the Coppice if it had been a fine day when we were there. It really is a great view from up there isn't it? There's nothing here to compare with it as it's as flat as a pancake. The only time you can see any hills here is on a clear day. You can see the Pennines and the TV mast at Winter Hill. On rare days you can see Barrow to the north, and to* the south the mountains in North Wales are visible, as is Anglesey. The trouble is that when it's so clear you can bet it's going to pour down for a week.

Must get back to the chemistry or I'll be up past midnight.

Still thinking of you.

All my love, L xxxxx

P.S. Here's a chemistry joke. What happened when oxygen went out with potassium? It went OK!

May 1966

Dear M,

This afternoon we had our annual day at the park, i.e., the school sports. They were rained off on Wednesday so we had them today in glorious sunshine. I was going to skive off as soon as they started but I was put on car park duty so it was a bit difficult.

I am trying to save some money so that I can go to the TT races in the Isle of Man in June. It's a special trip organised by a motorcycle paper going by boat from Liverpool and it's two thirds of the normal fare. If a gang of us go it should be fun.

Did you see that TV programme about growing up in America? One lad, about 18 or 19, made me laugh when he said that some boys there actually go out drinking beer, picking up girls and 'dirty things' like that. He seemed genuinely shocked by it! He ought to come to Blackpool on a Saturday night. That would really horrify him, wouldn't it? Mind you, there was one point in their favour; that is that nearly all of them have cars and you only have to be 16 to have a driving licence. To get one you only have to pass a simple, written examination.

Today is polling day for local elections. At junior school we always had a day off as the school was used as a polling station - those were the days, eh what, playing with building blocks, painting and making models out of plasticine and no homework.

I went to the dentist on Tuesday to have a tooth extracted. It certainly had roots cos the dentist nearly needed a crane to get the thing out and gallons of blood came pouring out. It was not a pretty sight.

It sounds as if you're really getting down to your revision. I keep thinking I should make a start but then I get distracted. After the exams are over I shall have to come over and see you. Who knows, I might even have got my bike going by then. If I have, I'll take you for a ride. Don't worry I'll drive very carefully with you on board.

So Caroline said she thought I looked Spanish. I've never been called that before although when people know that my dad's not English they do sometimes say they thought I looked a bit foreign.

Don't work too hard. All my love, L xxxxx

May 1966

Dear M,

Hope you got home all right. Next time you come, try and make sure you have a different driver so that I don't have to walk home.

Isn't the weather fab? When I took O-level we had Whit week off just before the start and the weather was so good that I did all my Latin revision on the sand hills. This morning I did some physics revision and learned all about Kundt's tube - masters always went beetroot coloured when they said that.

There's some motorbike racing on the TV this afternoon so I'll probably watch it instead of working. There's still plenty of time to do more cramming and you can have too much of a good thing.

Speaking of TV, did you see that film called **The Searchers**? I can remember that when I was about eight or nine years old my friends and I went to see it on three consecutive days because we thought it was so fab. I still quite like watching John Wayne films.

I've just switched on the TV and found out that Lancashire are being bowled out by Yorkshire. I'm not peeved because we're losing but because they're winning. By the way, who actually won the Wars of the Roses, them or us?

My ma reckoned that we might have been back to our house on Saturday night because I left the curtains shut. She later had two comments to make. One was why didn't I give you your coffee in one of our better cups and the other was why didn't I ask you how you liked the house. I reckon my ma is a bit of a snob but she won't admit it.

Looking forward to seeing you again soon.

Love, L xxxxx

*June 1966*

*Dear M,*

*You'll never guess where I ended up on Saturday night - in a Baptist tabernacle of all places. I was walking home from the Tower through the centre of town and a fab bird - er, sorry - a nice-looking young lady approached me and asked me if I would like a free cup of coffee. Since it was free and just round the corner I decided to go along - nothing ventured, nothing gained, I thought.*

*It was a poky sort of place with a number of circles of chairs and tables dotted here and there with one or two 'converted' people strategically placed at each table. They bleated away like Billy Graham himself, saying how lonely and sad they were before they met you know who and how he died for them on the cross and was their friend. I think I upset the 'converted one' next to me when I said that he couldn't have tried very hard to find friends in the first place and that he had taken the easy way out then I drank my coffee and left.*

*Last Monday we had the general studies paper. It wasn't too bad. I managed to write eight sides on how helicopters work and about as much again about Harold Wilson's lack of a Rhodesian policy. There was another question about comprehensive* education which would have suited you no end. I'll probably fail it again this year - yet another waste of three hours.

I don't like to admit it but I must say that I do like that Georgie Fame record, **Get Away**. The Yardbirds' and Animals' latest aren't bad either.

I saw that programme about holiday camps on TV. What exactly are you going to do there? I still haven't got a job but I can't say that I've really tried yet.

All my love, L xxxxx

*June 1966*

*Dear M,*

*Thank you for the fab letter.*

*I hope you're not suffering from exam blues.
So far all my exams have been far worse than I
expected so much so that I've been looking in the
papers to see what sort of jobs are going. I didn't
see anything but I'll keep looking.*

*I went on a rather tame pub crawl to Cleveleys on
Saturday but came home perfectly sober, probably as
none of us had much money so we had to spin out
the drinks.*

*I read an article on mental illness at weekend
and discovered that Tchaikovsky was homosexual
and a manic depressive with a dread of women
and sex. He had a disastrous marriage with a
nymphomaniac and constantly feared that his
head would fall off so when he was conducting
he held his head with one hand and the baton
with the other. Apparently a lot of artists are a bit
mental.*

*Those plays you have to do at school in your
drama competitions seem a riot. Have you ever had
to do any of the love scenes yourself?*

*I sorted my school bag out the other day. The
contents included a spark plug, a* **Castrol**

*Achievements* 1938 book, four motorcycle magazines, a crumpled packet of biscuits, a programme for the Manx Grand Prix and someone else's physics book.

I hear that **Which** did an article on contraceptives. I wonder how they tested them. I shouldn't have thought there would have been a shortage of volunteers!

Good luck in your remaining exams.

All my love, L xxxxx

June 1966

Dear M,

The weather seems to be holding out for a change. On Tuesday I actually sunbathed in the back garden. I let one of our rabbits free in the garden but unfortunately it escaped into the street. I must say that I got lots of funny looks when I was running around the street half-naked after a rabbit. It must have taken me at least twenty minutes to catch it. It's quite a big one, too, nearly the size of your dog.

I've got physics tomorrow afternoon but I'd rather write this letter to you than revise. When I'm in bed on the eve of an exam, millions of facts seem to be floating round in my head so much so that it's usually about 3am before I get to sleep. Until then I keep answering exam questions in my head. I feel that when I'm asleep knowledge oozes out of my ears and covers the floor so if I put cotton wool in my ears, I feel sure I'll remember more in the morning. At the moment I feel like I know less than I did last year so I haven't much confidence. It will soon be over then I'll forget about everything 'til a few days before the results. Enough of this morbid talk - worse things happen at sea, or so they say.

When I was walking home on Saturday night I thought how fab it must be to pile on to a coach with your friends and come somewhere like Blackpool for a night out and then go home on the coach literally full of spirits. Since I live here there's no great thrill in going to another. If I get in at Liverpool, I will definitely have a day trip to Blackpool.

Did you see in one of the Sunday papers the recommended amounts of pocket money we should get. It only went up to the age of 17. But it recommended ten bob! What can you do on ten bob? It's all right for those who don't drink, smoke or go out, i.e., all the brainy types in my form who never do anything but eat, sleep and drink chemistry, etc. They don't even know girls exist. It's not natural. Are there any like that at your school?

Can't say anything more except good luck in your remaining exams and don't worry too much as what's gonna be's gonna be and there's nothing you or I can do about it now.

All my love, L xxxxxxx

*June 1966*

*Dear M,*

*Well, it's all over for me now. I had a chemistry practical this morning which was a cinch. I don't think I will improve on last year's grades so I probably won't get in anywhere. I've been looking around to see what jobs are going and I think I might apply to the GPO. At 18 you start at £800 a year so it's worth trying for.*

*If it wasn't for the goggle box and Royal Ascot, I would be bored to tears just doing nothing all day. I have only picked one winner so far, so it's a good job I haven't put any money on. If the seamen's strike wasn't taking place, I would be off to the Isle of Man on the midnight boat tonight to see the TT races. I'll watch* **Top of the Pops** *instead - some anti-climax!*

*On Saturday I'll be at the Tower to celebrate the end of the exams. It's a fantastic feeling when you know for certain you've finished with homework, masters, uniforms, etc. The prospect of actually having to work for a living doesn't bring dread into my heart anymore. That's probably because I will be more free, have infinitely more cash and will probably living away somewhere.*

Recently the local rag has been full of letters complaining about the lack of teenage morals, their bad behaviour and lack of respect, etc. It always makes me angry with the rash generalisations about young people. The majority do not behave like the very small minority who actually do go around smashing up places and beating up old ladies. What gets me most is when they say everyone would be a better person after they had a spell in the army (National Service). Speaking of the army, have you ever seen a play on TV which shows the army in a good light, as I haven't? Have you ever considered joining any of the forces?

I sent off to Castrol for some free stuff and received a piece of paper which had a heading 'Free Lubrication for your Friends'. I wonder which parts need lubricating!

Well, that's about it for now.

Lots of love, L xxxxx

P.S. If you come to the Tower on Saturday you know where to find me.

*July 1966*

*Dear M,*

*I've left school at last so you can't call me a callow schoolboy anymore. Unfortunately, I am now swelling the ranks of the unemployed which won't please Harold W much. This morning I have been to numerous places in the search for a summer job. I could have got one at a bookie's office. The woman said I could have the job before she told me the wage. The hourly rate wasn't bad but it would only have been for a couple of days a week. If you hear of any jobs going at Butlin's in Pwhelli, write and tell me and I'll come and join you.*

*Blackpool town centre was like a ghost town last night. It was deserted probably because there was a World Cup match on TV. We watched in a pub and England won 2-1 against France.*

*I came off my motorbike yesterday. I was flashing round a country lane and hit some cow dung. Surprisingly it's more lethal than black ice. My bike was all right but the thickness of my skin in a certain area decreased considerably. I'll have to show you some time.*

*Last Friday was my last day at school and I was quite surprised that some of the masters were genuinely sincere in wishing us good luck for the* future. The boss invited us to Speech Day and told us all about the Old Boys Association. Will you become an old girl of your place?

Do you think going to college will change you? Some of my friends who left last year seem to have quietened down and become more responsible which was unexpected. I can't see it changing me that much.

I'll check the evening paper tonight to see if there are any jobs going. I'm almost stony broke so I really need to find something full-time as soon as possible. It seems that girls have the advantage as there are usually more jobs for them advertised in shops, catering and hotels. I'll keep looking so wish me luck.

Hope your job is going well. Let me know when you are back home and I'll try to come over to see you.

Still thinking of you, L xxxxx

*July 1966*

*Dear M,*

*This morning I have been all over the place looking for a job but still no luck.*

    *I had a rotten time on Saturday night. I arrived at the usual meeting place but I was late and no one was there. I went to the Tower but couldn't find any mates so I had a pint and went home.*

    *I've got an application form for the Fleet Air Arm. There are such gems as 'Do you still possess your left testicle?' Apparently, you can get in with one lung but if one leg is shorter than the other you can't - probably because the uniform won't fit.*

    *Yesterday I bought one of those plastic kits. It was raining so it was something to do. Even though I say it myself, it's a masterpiece and the painting of it is superb. I might have to go and get another one.*

    *Last week one of my friends passed his driving test so we went for a celebration drive. There were five of us in an ancient, battered Ford. It was a bit of a wreck and floated all over the road when the wind blew. We had a radio with us so we enjoyed a rowdy sing-song as we drove along. After a nine-point three-point turn, the back wheels went into a ditch and we all struggled to push it out. At the moment,*

I'm 'off' motorbikes and 'on' cars. I can't wait to drive and have my own car.

I've just heard a great record on Radio Caroline. It's called **The More I See You** by Joy Marshall. Have you heard it?

That's all for now.

All my love, L xxxxx

*July 1966*

*Thanks for the letter. Don't get too fed up of the place as you've now got one less week to work. The security spot checks sound a bit of a riot. Do they turn a blind eye to the staff's chalets?*

*I've got a job at last. It's general labouring renovating a house and converting it into flats. I've had plenty of experience of that sort of work because my dad does sweet f.a. about the house nowadays.*

*My friend's faith in women drivers took a nosedive yesterday when one of them flashed out of an entry into the back of his dad's car. His old man was not best pleased. I think women drivers are usually more careful than men and generally have less accidents. Do you want to learn to drive?*

*I don't know where we can go tonight because one of our number has a gang after him all because of some trivial matter - a girl of course! He's very chicken and doesn't want to go to any of the popular places in Blackpool so we'll probably end up in Cleveleys.*

*Yet another of my friends has said goodbye to freedom as he's getting engaged next week. He's well and truly hooked because she's only the second girl he's ever been out with. My friend's older brother went the same way as well. He had his first girlfriend* at 15, married her at 18 and now has two kids. When I see him he has no energy and looks like a typical hen-pecked husband.

I don't fancy getting married. I'd sooner have a succession of women with whom I can 'live in sin'. When you have a problem, you can then just part and find someone else without the trouble of a divorce. It may sound a bit harsh but it's how I feel.

The meals at Butlin's sound similar to those at ATC camp - greasy fry-ups and chips with everything and the tea's so strong you can stand your spoon up in it.

The weather has been fantastic so if it keeps up I will get a fab tan. Hope the weather in Wales is good. Will you be watching the World Cup final on Saturday? I probably will.

That's all for now.

All my love, L xxxxx

August 1966

Dear M,

Hope things are going well in Pwllheli. One of the students working on our site was going to work at your camp as a chef. He was with two others and only stayed there for five hours before they left. They didn't like the look of the accommodation, food and the place generally so they left. The management wasn't too pleased. I hope you and Hilary are coping.

Last week three of us cleaned a thousand bricks, it nearly drove us mental. Every one of them was marked 'Enfield Plastic Accrington'. Someone told me that because they are so strong, they used Accrington bricks in the foundations of the Empire State Building as well as in those of Blackpool Tower. I don't know if it's true or not.

The language at work is very crude. Everything is described with a four letter word with the suffixes 'ing', 'er' or 'ker'. The work is not too hard because we've done all the heavy stuff. It's better than working in a factory as it's varied and you have to be prepared to do anything from overhauling a cement mixer to painting bedrooms.

Sometimes I eat at the local chip shop with the other students. It's a decaying place run by three spinsters each aged over 60. They have run the place since the 1920s and are always saying how easy modern youth have it, not like the old days. I think they quite like us and they often give us extra chips if we ask them nicely.

Most of the men there are sex-mad and are constantly relating their sexual experiences which, in my opinion, is a load of bull. As in common with all building sites, work comes to a complete standstill when any reasonable looking female goes past as she is met by a barrage of mostly crude comments and wolf whistles - not the most mature or appropriate sort of behaviour.

That's all for now. Looking forward to seeing you when you get back.

Still thinking of you.

Love, L xxxxx

September 1966

Dear M,

I was to have spent my last day at work today but all this morning and most of last night I've been sick as a dog and had the Bombay you-know-whats. I am feeling better now but I really was rough - and I hadn't even had a drink!

Last Sunday I was on my way to a scramble on my bike and got caught in one of those monsoons which seem to be a feature of our English summers, with the result that my engine was more or less drowned. It took a couple of hours to dry out so I reached home when I eventually got it going.

Discotheques seem to be popping up all over the place. We went to a new one last Saturday. It was about the size of the Rainbow Room in the Tower but more square if you see what I mean. It was half a dollar to get in and the music was provided by a jukebox in the corner. The beer wasn't bad and not too dear. I've heard that *Revolver* LP. It's quite good, especially **Here There and Everywhere** and **Tomorrow will Tell**. What about that record by Dave Dee, Dozy, etc **Bend it** - pretty good, isn't it? It's **Zorba's Dance** with words.

I'm going to the motorbike races in the Isle of Man next Monday, overnight by boat from Liverpool.

There's always a fab atmosphere on those boats to the island. I suppose I'll spend most of my time in the 2$^{nd}$ class saloon - sounds rather cheap doesn't it?

That's all for now.

Lots of love, L xxxxxxx

P.S. I think I've got in Liverpool.

September 1966

Dear M,

I've definitely got in at Liverpool. Next week I'll be tramping about Liverpool trying to find digs. Unfortunately, I was too late to get into the halls of residence.

I went to the Isle of Man with some friends on Monday to see the Manx Grand Prix. We went by boat from Liverpool. It was very rough-going and many of the passengers spent the journey with their heads hanging over the side of the ship. I was all right but one of my friends looked a bit green when we arrived in Douglas. The racing was very good and we watched from a corner near a pub which was open all day.

On the way back we chatted to some girls from Liverpool who were - wait for it - chalet maids at Pontins. They quite liked it and they told us that some chalets cost 17 guineas a week. Who in their right mind would pay 17 guineas to stay at a holiday camp?

I went whippet racing on Friday and won over £3 on bets. There's a lot of fiddling at small meetings and my friend spotted one that was running under a false name which had got a good starting handicap. It won at five to one which are very good odds as they rarely exceed two or two and a half to one. I had ten bob on it so I did all right. I won seventy shillings on the horses the other weekend so it was quite profitable - a much easier way of earning money than working, if your luck's in that is.

No one's going out tonight so I'm staying in. I'll watch the **Last Night of the Proms**. It's usually quite good especially at the end when **Rule Britannia** is played. Malcolm Sargeant invariably seems to really enjoy himself along with the audience.

When do you go away to college? I go around 5<sup>th</sup> October so the sands of my sheltered life are rapidly running out to be replaced by the big, wide, not always so wonderful outside world.

I'm going to a stag party next week as one of my friends has got to get married. I don't know how they're going to live because both sets of parents have more or less disowned them which seems a bit unjust. He is only an apprentice and she won't be able to work much longer being pregnant. Ah well, that's life I suppose.

Will you be coming over to Blackpool any time? Please let me know and we can meet up at the Tower.

All my love, L xxxxx

September 1966

Dear M,

Are you feeling excited about the prospect of going away to college soon? I'm not, well not yet. I probably will next Saturday night. I'm going up on Sunday. I got digs on Thursday. It's quite near Anfield and Goodison Park football grounds so that will be convenient. It takes about 25 minutes on the bus to get to university from where I live. Please send me your address. Will you be in digs or residence?

I've not done much lately. I've gone fishing a few times but caught absolutely nothing. One day we went up to Ribchester, but it was so warm and sunny we abandoned the fishing and just sunbathed by the river.

This morning I cleared out all the junk I have accumulated over the last 18 years. There seemed to be tons of it. I got rid of hundreds of various motorcycle magazines and another 150 about aviation. They now lie outside in a big pile in the hope that the dustmen will take them away.

Another of my friends is getting married on Saturday. It seems quite fashionable nowadays, doesn't it? On Friday we are having a bit of a binge / stag do. If you cast your mind back to that fateful night, last October, when we first met, he was the one with me. A year ago he was free and now? I'll reserve judgement! We're clubbing together to get him a wedding present but have no idea what to buy. Any ideas?

All my love, L xxxxx


P.S. I'll come up and see you on Thursday. I seem to remember you saying that it would be all right. It will be nice to see you again so I'll come around the same time.

Love, L xxxxx

October 1966

Dear M,

Thanks for your letter. Soon you too will be living in this great northern city of Liverpool. Are you looking forward to it?

My grant hasn't come through yet so I'm on the brink of insolvency, not to worry as I've written a begging letter to my ma.

I don't seem to be worked very hard and I get Wednesday, Friday and alternate Thursday afternoons off which isn't too bad. I seem to have lots of maths which is a bind. I haven't had much work yet but I have a feeling that I will have plenty by weekend.

What are you going to study besides education? You didn't seem too sure when I saw you last.

The Union building is really something with a big bar and dances every Saturday night. It also has a large canteen and a new sports centre.

Most of my lunchtimes have been spent in city centre cafes. I've discovered that Lime Street Station has the best café for a cheap meal. Altogether there are six from my old school here. I've made new friends quite easily since there are only about twenty freshers in our department. They all seem all right and we have a laugh when we go into town.

My roommate also seems all right and we have been down to the local pub a couple of times. The pub is called The Hermitage and serves draught Double Diamond.

I no longer get lost when in town and I've got into the habit of always sticking my hand out when the bus comes. If you forget they'll never stop for you.

I tried out the baths in the new sports centre and they're really great and free of course. My roommate tried to buy a pair of swimming trunks in town this morning but he couldn't get any. Apparently they're out of season!

One of my friends from back home is living a couple of doors from where George Harrison used to live and that chap David Garrick, who sings **Mrs Applebee**, lived a few streets from my new residence. I have also discovered the location of the Cavern but have heard widely varying reports on what it's like.

I haven't got my scarf yet but when I do, I'll dirty it a bit so I won't look too much like a fresher.

That's all for now. No doubt we'll have lots to talk about next time we meet.

All my love, L xxxxxxx

P.S. Hope to see and hear from you soon.

P.P.S. If you phone, please leave it 'til after 6pm as I may not be back.

November 1966

Dear M,

I've been trying to phone you but the line seems to be permanently engaged so I've put pen to paper again for a change. I really enjoyed our night in Kirkby and at the Carters. We must do it again soon. It's very handy having a pub right on your doorstep and the beer's not bad either.

When I was in town, I saw a poster for a play at the Everyman and the title intrigued me. It's called **Little Malcolm and his Struggle against the Eunuchs** and it sounds weirdly interesting. Now I'm solvent we could go next Friday if you like then we could go to Pier Head for one of those fab hotdogs.

I was in the Union coffee bar this morning and they were playing one of your favourites, the Beach Boys **Good Vibrations** and I was thinking about you. We've known each other over a year now and written I don't know how many letters to each other and now we are living in the same town - well almost.

I'll go and post this letter and take the landlady's dog for a walk with A and we might just call in the nearest pub for a quick half.

Don't work too hard.

All my love, L xxxxxxxx

P.S. Phone me at the digs tomorrow after six and let me know about Friday.

See you soon xxxx

December 1966

Dear M,

The bus journey home was freezing cold but it was really nice looking out of the window from Liverpool to Preston. The lights of Kirkby (silent tears drop from the heart) looked spectacular. The sky was sort of sooty black with orange streaks on the right side of the bus and the lights of the TV mast at Winter Hill were almost rivalling the Tower back home. On the other side the sky was all sorts of colours, red, orange, yellow, mixed into the clouds, which were silhouetted against the dark blue sky. When the bus approached Preston, the sky had a warm yellow haze as if the town was on fire. Altogether it was very colourful and picturesque journey.

In a way I'm glad the bus came early so I wouldn't see you upset because you know how it affects me - all the same it's great to know that you really care for me.

Please write and tell me when you can come over to see me. I'm missing you already.

All my love, L xxxxx

December 1966

Dear M,

I hope work isn't getting you down too much. I suppose it's all right when the weather's fine but at least you can sometimes get an early finish when your delivery's done. I'm writing this in my break in the canteen which, still inside the building, is the farthest point from where I'm working. By the time you've walked back to the sorting office you need another break to recover.

When I was sorting yesterday, I came across your letter and I let it go through the usual channels but when I got home at night it hadn't arrived. I assume it will be there when I get back. I get paid today (hurray!) for the first two days that I worked. There are only a few students doing sorting, one of whom I used to regularly trample on every year when we played rugby against his school. I never did like him. He's at Durham University now.

This morning I was press-ganged into working until ten tonight unloading mail bags at the station. I think I've got to do it tomorrow as well – I'll just think of the extra money.

My ma said that my pa reckons that I drink too much. Whether it's intended as a hint to cut down or not I don't know. I reckon he's just jealous because I could annihilate him in a drinking contest.

I'm beginning to get a bit peeved on account of some of the derogatory remarks about my beard so it might not be there next time I see you.

As always, still thinking of you.

All my love, L xxxxxxxx

December 1966

Dear M,

I've just been at the pub with some other casual postal workers There was no work for us so we were sent home and instead decided to call in for a pre-Christmas tipple.

The party scene here is a bit feeble. I've not heard of any yet and it's nearly Christmas Eve. I have decided to get you something _very_ useful for Christmas instead of that perfume, Blue Grass, wasn't it? This has nothing to do with my financial situation of course.

I sorted a letter for your street today, number 11, and quite a few for that place which always tickles me - Oswaldtwistle. Did you get my card? I hope so as it seems a miracle that anything actually gets delivered, doesn't it?

All my love, L xxxxx

P.S. Thanks for the card. Guess how many cards I sent!

P.P.S. I shall give you your present the next time I see you - no need to get me anything.

P.P.P.S. Your letter just arrived. Of course I would like to come so I'll probably arrive at your house between 6 and 7 tomorrow. If for any reason you're out please leave Caroline's address and I'll find my way there somehow.

January 1967

Dear M,

Happy New Year and Happy Birthday. Hope you got my card. As usual it wasn't a very inspired choice but it's the thought that counts.

I really enjoyed being with you at the party at Caroline's and I hope the budgie has fully recovered from Keith's attentions. Somehow budgie on toast does not sound that appetising but it was funny.

Unfortunately, no one wanted to go out on New Year's Eve so I went to the Tower to drink the new year in, in the hope of finding someone I might know. At the bar I got into a deep conversation with two engaged couples. We ended up discussing marriage. Of course you know my views on that. I must have put them forward convincingly because they didn't seem all that sure about going through with it after I'd finished explaining my point of view.

Noel managed to get some free tickets for the Mecca so we went last night. It was Golden Disc Night. There was no group or anything just a twit of a DJ putting on lousy records. The drinks were 4d a pint cheaper than the last time we went so progress of some sort has been made.

Did you watch **Till Death us do Part** the other day? It was really funny when they were talking about sex before marriage and Alf called his son-in-law a 'randy Scouse git'. The wallpapering bit was hilarious too.

I've entered Radio Caroline Cash Casino again but I haven't decided what to do with the winnings. I've decided on my holiday though - Rimini. I can't remember where I said I was going previously, probably Rome. Now it's Rimini on the Adriatic coast and you can come with me if I win.

I've got a new beard style now. It's more slim line and Manfred Mann-ish and very handsome it makes me look too, as does my new shirt. My ma called it my 'shirt of many colours'. Didn't someone in the Bible have something like that? Was it David or Jacob - not sure as I'm not into that stuff. I'll take it to Liverpool with me. Hope you like it. Dying to get back to you and the Pool of Life

As ever, all my love, L xxxxxxxx

P.S. Can't wait to be with you next Friday night in Liddypool xxx

February 1967

Dear M,

It seems strange not seeing you Saturday and Sunday. I hope your mum is feeling better after her operation. I'll miss you but as it's my first experience of Panto week at least there's plenty going on.

On Thursday I went to Birkenhead to sell even more **Panto Sphinx** magazines. Did the same on Friday. I sold even more on Saturday with my roommate. He was more interested in football so he only saw a few of the floats before he went to the match. I carried on watching the parade. It was very good and I got a ride on our float. If you had been with me you could have got on as well. Our float was a ten-foot high beer mug and a 'Bat Boy'.

There was a sort of fair next to St George's Hall with lots of stalls. I bought **Ape and Essence** by Aldous Huxley, from a second-hand book stall as it's been a play I enjoyed on TV. I suppose it has a deep meaning but to me it's just a good story.

In the evening we called in the cocktail bar next to the Adelphi. It was full of dubious looking ladies but good for a laugh. Then my friend's incessant love for football meant we had to find a pub with a TV to watch **Match of the Day**.

If I'm still here next year I'm going to be on a float and dress up for Panto Day. In the crowd I saw quite a few girls wearing Kirkby scarves but none I recognised. There were loads of students from Bangor of all places, trying to sell their inferior magazines.

I've really missed seeing you this weekend. Ring me when you're back in Kirkby. You can leave a message if I'm not back.

All my love, L xxxxx

March 1967

Dear M,

I'm home safe and sound and I hope you are too.

My ma and pa are snoring away and I'm downstairs writing to you. Please excuse the pencil but I can't find a pen anywhere.

After seeing us in the Tower Lounge, my ma said how nice you seemed and how well you and her would get on if you had time to really get to know each other. Not sure what that was all about but that's what she said.

I'll bet you'd look good in one of those floppy-type trouser suits. I saw a woman on TV wearing one and I'll bet you would look great wearing a similar one. By the way, you looked great in your new panties last Saturday night in Liverpool.

There were some pictures of models in the paper the other day. They were awful - all skinny like Twiggy. They'd got horrible legs, all parallel and about six inches apart - not a patch on you.

Looking forward to seeing you soon.

I love you, L xxxxx

P.S. It's now 3am and I can't sleep. The reason is because I keep thinking about you. I know what the best night cap of all would be but you're not here.

I've just read some of your most recent letters and I keep thinking of how we're going to be apart these holidays. The prospect is dreadful. Let's try to see each other as often as possible until we're both back in Liverpool. I'll try to sleep now.

All my love, L xxxxx

April 1967

Dear M,

Well, what happened to the letter you were going to write on Wednesday night? Was it you I was waving to or your gatepost?

I wonder if our dam stood up to the downpour on Thursday or if it was all washed away. I've got the photos and a lot were failures but the one of you down by the river is fantastic. I'll let you see them on Saturday. Needless to say, the ones you took of me are great. You seem to reveal new and exciting features of my undoubted handsomeness.

Guess what. The post has just arrived (1pm) and there was your promised letter. Nothing will ever change the way I feel about you. Whenever I'm on my own all I can think about is you. I don't know what I would do without you because now you are such a large part of my existence. Nearly everything seems to centre about you and it's doubly marvellous because I never thought it happened and to me as well. We'll soon be back in Liverpool and we'll be content again. With you I always feel secure and happy and I hate anything to intrude or take it away from us, even if it's just going back to the digs on Sunday nights. I hate leaving your loving arms as I feel that's the place I belong. That last bit might sound a bit corny but it's what I feel deep inside. Like Pete said, we must be in love.

Love you forever, L xxxxxxx

P.S. I read an article the other day. It said that Pisceans tend to ramble on but always manage to get down on paper the affection they feel for the person they're writing to. For Capricorns it said that their friends should never worry if a letter isn't answered promptly.

Love you, L xxxxxxxxx

*April 1967*

*Dear M,*

*Just a few lines to say:*

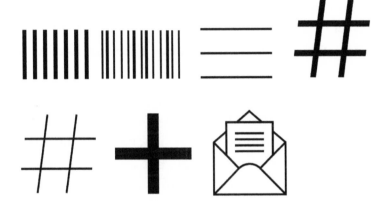

*I LOVE YOU XXXXXXXXXX*

May 1967

Dear M,

How arst thee, fine feeling, I hope? I have just upgot and am now stoning to the listening Rollers LP. S'il vous plait ecrude the script as I am not too well at feeling. I hab a heaby colb and can harbly breab on a count of nobe being up blocked.

I am pensing that you can't understand eni of this crapthyiclacity which rescribes it wishingly well. As I compose this epilepsy the Rolling Brickheads are singeing *you can make it if you try* and shorely was never a jester word truer in sprocket. *In my lonely womb* I think of you every day, *all of the night and all of the day* (a few song bits there).

I have just been truly inspired by reading **The Penguin John Lennon**, which is **In His own Write** and **A Spaniard in the Works** combined. I think most of his poetry is up to my standard especially **Good Dog Nigel** and **I'm a Moldy Moldy Man**

How dare they out cut some of **Pop of the Tops**? Only foobtall can take president over **Tops of the Popsicles and Momsicles.**

It was great talking to you on Thursday and I'm really looking forward to seeing you on Saturday morning in Kirkby - pretend to be asleep.

Loaves off Fluff, L xxxxxxxxx

P.S. I'm now reading about the General Erection won by Harrassed Wilsod abetted by the Trade Onions xxxxx

May 1967

Dear M,

It was great talking to you tonight even if it was only for a few minutes and I'm dying to see you again on Tuesday. Last weekend it was fantastic being able to stay in bed together all that time and make love as we did - what a nice phrase that is! I wish we were in a house, just the two of us. It would be heaven on earth having all the time for each other. I don't know what I'd do if we don't live together, not now anyway.

You remember at college we were talking about me being faithful well I shall be forever. I love you, respect you and have such high regard for you that I don't want anyone else but you, only you. That must sound terribly possessive but it's the truth.

When I come to see you and we go out together it's wonderful. I think our love is not pure habit and it's to our mutual satisfaction. If it was pure habit then I wouldn't love you and you'd just be a sort of object or possession of mine but I love you and that's what makes our relationship so wonderful.

I don't know what I would do without you as I love you so much. You were right when you said that we needed sex and each other. Sex is such a marvellous thing between us because we are sharing so much. It is an outlet for all our worries and problems. When we are in bed together and naked, we are together just being ourselves which is what everyone should try to be, don't you think? Being next to each other 'naked', so to speak, we are perfectly honest and frank with each other. We show our complete love and affection for each other.

I think sex without love is meaningless and pointless. It's because we love each other so much that we want to show our love both physically and emotionally. The effect it has on us when we see each other enjoying our love so much makes it so meaningful. We need it because we need each other so much. Life without you would be pointless, I'm sure.

I wish I could express myself really well so that I could tell you more amply how I feel about you and love you but I hope you can tell how I feel when we are making love. It's such a marvellous thing.

As you now know I have never slept with anyone except you. I never thought it could be so desirable and beautiful. I couldn't imagine I would ever feel like this about anyone but I love you and I always will.

This must be the most passionate letter I have ever written to you but I always feel like this about you. I think about you almost all the time, in fact I've thought about you constantly since we first met. I can remember thinking about you when I was at school and we just used to write to each other. Now I think of you, yes, constantly because I think so much of you.

Dying to see you on Tuesday.

All my love, L

xxxxxxxx

P.S. I love you. I love you. I love you. xxxxxxx

*July 1967*

*Dear M,*

I suppose you are nearly home now. I'm going to miss our time in Liverpool over the summer. Do you remember that song **It might as well rain until September**? I used to have the record. Well, I heard it on the radio this morning and it brought a tear to my eye. '... For all the fun I'll have while you're so far away - It might as well rain until September'.

Do you know what I would like to do? Go walking with you in the pouring rain just wearing some light clothes along a deserted beach or through a wood. With you the rain wouldn't bother me at all. It's funny but just lately whenever it has rained, I have got an urge to go out in it, running around in it and generally being silly and singing, of course.

This time last year who could have imagined that it would be like this between us? I'm so glad though. I love you and I think I need you now. I really want you for my own. That does sound rather possessive, but I do.

I will miss you but let's hope the time will soon pass until we're both back in the Pool. I do hope we get that flat so you can come and stay with me.

<u>Eve to Adam under the apple tree</u>
Adam, do you love me?
<u>Adam</u>
Sure do, Eve. There ain't nobody else.
I could never care about anyone else the way I care about you. I don't want anyone but you.
Sorry it's so short, love. Don't want to miss the post.
All my love, L xxxxxx

P.S. Please come and see me ASAP xxxxx

July 1967

Dear M,

I think they believed me about going to a party. My dad just said, 'Oh, oh lover boy's back,' then just started to ramble on about the way I behaved being at university saying he didn't want me to be like that. He said it was all up to me so there was nothing to argue about. From the mood he was in it would have been pointless arguing with him anyway. He said he didn't want to see you in his house for a long time and reckoned we were seeing far too much of each other. I don't think he likes you, but I do and that's what counts. He still wants to be in control of what I do and I think he sees you as a threat to that.

I've heard that record **San Francisco** by Scott Mackenzie. It's really good but it does remind me of another record. As soon as we get back to Liverpool we can have our own 'love-in' even if we don't put the flowers in our hair.

Guess what? I've shaved off my beard. When I was shaving, I thought I would see what I would look like with a goatee. Well I looked strange so I shaved it off but I've still got my tash. I don't look too bad, just a bit like a lawyer in a cowboy film.

This afternoon I'll resume my seemingly endless quest of finding a job.

Please don't worry about what my dad said. I won't. The ten months since I went to Liverpool have meant more to me than what all the riches in the world could buy.

Great weekend, wasn't it?

Love you, L xxxxxxx (at least 1000-fold)

*July 1967*

*Dear M,*

Yet another bed-inspired letter and yet another day job hunting. Did you see the Turtles on **Top of the Pops** tonight? They were good, weren't they? Didn't think much of Tom Jones or the Tremeloes though.

I had a fantastic dream last night. We had left college and university and we hadn't seen each other for some time (we're not going to let that happen, are we?) and I took you up to the Lakes in my car. It was marvellous weather of course, birds singing in the trees , blue skies and very hot. We came across a pub (surprise, surprise) high in a valley overlooking one of the lakes and we stopped for a meal. We were so impressed with the place that we stayed the night there together (four-poster bed of course). We lived happily ever after in the cottage next to the pub getting married at Gretna Green when we were 70. I don't know what we lived on but we managed. There was a dog in it somewhere - probably a replica of Shandy.

There was a job in tonight's paper for a general help in a hotel. These are usually about £10 per week but this one was to live-in, which I'm not too sure about. There was another possibility at a biscuit factory in Kirkham. I'll keep looking. I'm sure something will crop up.

I'll come over on Saturday after I've checked the evening paper so I'll probably be there around seven. Looking forward to seeing you then.

All my love, L xxxxx

P.S. Don't forget that seductive letter you promised me. Love you xxxx

*July 1967*

*Dear M,*

*Thank you for the fab letter.*

*I hope you have a good first day at work. First days are always hectic but you soon get used to it. Finally got a job in the kitchens at the B Hotel on the prom and I've now served two days of my sentence at the sink. It's not too bad now I've got into the swing of things. Another 12 people came to stay this afternoon so there are now 50. I never realised that people would use so many plates for every meal. It's bad enough washing up at home but this is ridiculous, but I need the money. The boss is a good chap and he tries makes sure that tips are shared with all the staff.*

*I got absolutely soaked on my way home yesterday on my sub-super-sonic moped. It's a <u>Hardly Davidson</u>. You will have to see me on it, all togged up with goggles and helmet and ready for action.*

*Did you see that article in the Sunday paper about the hippies in London? I'd love to go to one of those Hyde Park 'be-ins' or one of those freak-outs where you all go in an aircraft hangar with loud music and throw mud and water at each other. It would be great wallowing around in it. Apparently in San Francisco it's the Summer of Love* and we should all be making love not war - sounds all right to me!

Do you think what I write in these letters is sometimes silly or too serious? I doubt if anyone could imagine me feeling this way about anybody, let alone writing such letters. It doesn't bother me at all and I love reading your letters.

Thanks again for the fab letter.

All my love, L xxxxx

P.S. Why did the hippie drown? He was far out, man!

July 1967

Dear M,

I'm getting sick of work as it's absolutely packed. It's the only hotel I've seen with a 'No Vacancy' sign. I'm glad to hear that you're doing some college work as well as packing Christmas cards. I'd better do some before I go back so I'll have some inkling of what the lecturers are on about.

The boss said I could have Thursday and Friday off and I can't wait for the 7:15 from North. In a way it seems nice to finish work and then get a train to see you. I know we can't sleep together and that I have to go home the next evening but I'd come just for the day even if I had to get the 11pm bus from Blackburn. I wish we were on our own working and living together. It's worth waiting for isn't it?

I had a haircut today on my way home. Don't flinch - it's still long at the back. I went to a place called Leslie's Salon. Had a hair wash, cut and blow dry finished off with - wait for it - COSSACK hairspray and all for eight bob. Don't worry I only had a trim and the blow wave dropped out with getting wet on the way back.

Dying to see you.

All my love, L xxxxxxx

P.S. I look at that photo of you every night before I go to sleep and I'm sure I drop off with a smile on my face - no sexy dreams yet.

*August 1967*

Dear M,

I should have realised that they had been to see your parents when they told me where the Reliant had broken down.

When I got home from work my ma was in with your letter on the table. She said that I ought to read it in case there was anything important in it. I knew something was wrong as she usually leaves the letters in my bedroom. I then found out they had been up to your place while you were here with me in Blackpool. She said that all four of them were worried about us. They didn't say that we weren't to see each other - not that that would have made any difference. There was no mention of that weekend when they came back early from holiday. There were no rows or anything. My dad came home later but didn't say a word.

Nothing will make any difference to how I feel about you. I love you so much. I feel so concerned for you and I hope they aren't making life at home unbearable.

My ma also said that your parents were very nice and were very worried about you. I think they are overdoing the protective parent bit. It's as if they are more concerned about our education than our feelings. We are old enough to make our own decisions about what we do. I wish we were a million miles away from all this. It makes me unhappy to know that you're unhappy too.

If they did say we couldn't see each other, they couldn't stop us unless they chained me to a lamp post or something. Please come on Saturday so we can have a talk about everything and be together.

Please try to keep your chin up, stiff upper lip and all that and remember that I'll always love you.

All my love, L

xxxxxxx

August 1967

Dear M,

Good news - phoned up the B Hotel and got in for next Monday. The woman even said that we could have an early breakfast before catching the plane.

Not so good news - coming home from work on my moped I was approached by a policeman. He noticed no tax, no test and no L plates so I'll get summonsed. It's my own fault and it will probably cost me about £5, worse luck. I think I'll have to sell it to get the money. So now you know another bloke on the police books.

Great news about the hotel. I wonder if it will be the same room as last time. I gave your surname but I didn't give an address. Let's have a great time in Blackpool and the Isle of Man and forget about anyone or anything else.

I love you and can't wait for Monday.

All my love, L xxxxxxx

August 1967

Dear M,

Thanks for coming to see me. I would have been ever so lost if you had not come. It was a great evening. It's always great when I'm with you. The film was good, wasn't it? I've just been admiring myself in the mirror, full length, nude, and I have come to the conclusion that I am nearly as handsome as Dr Zhivago.

I suppose you will now be nearly home. I wish I could be with you - memories of those much too infrequent occasions when I came home with you on the coach.

I think our only real home is Liverpool. If people have never been like we have been they have no idea at all what life is all about. They must have lots of preconceived ideas to which they stick without faltering. That's all wrong. Decisions depend so much upon changing feelings, events and states of mind. Future decisions cannot be ruled by past, fixed ideas. That's a philosophy, I suppose.

It's all building up inside me for Monday. I can't wait to finish work and dash down to the Coliseum to meet you. It's going to be great. Just imagine two nights in the hotel and a return to our island.

I love you. I love you. I love you. Words can't describe adequately how I feel about you and the important part you play in my life.

All my love, L xxxxx

P.S. Don't forget the ring and your watch.

I love you. See you at 7 at the Coliseum xxxxx

September 1967

Dear M,

I don't know what happened when you got back. I hope everything was all right. My pa seemed convinced that we had been having a couple of days in Blackpool, that is until he saw all my souvenirs and rock. You'll come Saturday, won't you? I'm missing you terribly and can't wait to see you again.

We always seem to be plagued with bad weather when we manage to get away together. Still, it doesn't spoil our enjoyment. I really enjoyed being with you. It was much, much better than going with my mates as I have done for the last two years. I wish we were there now in the dockside pub at Peel or sheltering in the rain at Laxey or better still at the B Hotel. We'll have to go again soon. It was great holding you in my arms or just tickling you, trying to make you hysterical or even just doing the crossword together.

I've been reading poetry again. This is by Emily Dickinson and it's very appropriate:

'Wild nights - wild nights were I with thee, wild nights should be our luxury. Futile - the winds - to a heart in port - Done with the compass - Done with

the chart! Rowing in Eden - Ah the sea! Might
I moor - Tonight in thee!'
   Looking forward to many more 'wild nights'.
   I love you, L xxxxxx

September 1967

Dear M,

My dad had another talk with me tonight and I managed to stand up for myself, no tears or anything, and I was very calm about it. I said that at this time he shouldn't tell me what he wanted me to do but he still thinks he should 'til I've finished my education. I said that at my age it was up to me to decide what I want to do. If I keep saying that he will eventually realise that I am right and not still just his schoolboy son. I think my ma agrees with me and that's part of the battle. Anyway, when I see you at weekend. I can give you the latest developments on the situation. You were right, of course, when you reckoned I should stick up for myself - thanks, you're a love for it.

I feel a bit lonely at the moment. I think about the nights we spent in the boarding house. It was really marvellous that last time, wasn't it? After I realised the great love and pleasure we had just then shared, I felt wonderful. It was something really special.

All this is making me feel very frustrated. I can't wait to be back together with you in Liverpool again.

Thinking of you constantly.

All my love, L xxxxx

114

September 1967

Dear M,

Thanks for the two fab letters. The funny one was simply great. I got puzzle 2 right but not puzzle 1.

I got my grant form back. The swines have reduced my grant by twenty shillings! I'll have a word or two to say to my local councillor about that. I think he's on the education committee.

It's really busy here at the moment, must be something to do with all those sparkly lights that keep coming on. How can we abolish or rather deter all visitors to the Pool? - Number 2 Pool. The Black one not the Liver one. There is only one notable exception, a girl I happen to love called, er, er, oh it's just slipped my mind. Ah well, it will come to me later. We could say it always rains in Blackpool. Trouble is they already know that and they still keep coming by the bus- and train-load. We could demolish the Tower - the tall structure not the ballroom for very sentimental reasons.

It was great on Thursday. I only wish we could have had more time together - now I've remembered the name of that girl - it's you, M. ML, the girl who means more to me than anything else in the world.

What does 'sagacity' mean? A poor science undergraduate like me, with a moustache, who is completely absorbed in a world of postulates, hypotheses, abstract principles, facts and figures (37C/26/36) can't possibly have any chance of knowing these rare and meaningful words carefully chosen to fit the context of the fundamental connotation or philosophy, can he? I.e., this illiterate but very sexy yobbo.

My fingers are entwined around Fred at the moment. He's throbbing with passion and is very frustrated. He sends you his regards and hopes he'll see you soon.

I love you, L

Xxxxxxxxx I mean to collect these

October 1967

Dear M,

It really cheered me up when I got your fantastic letter and I can't wait to see you on Saturday. It's now nearly midnight and I still have lots of work to do. It's much harder than last year but I suppose I'll manage.

The move went all right and now we're in the caravan at Formby. I can't remember the address properly but I think it would be better if you kept on writing to the Union so that I can get your letters before I go back to the van in the evenings.

Let's go to the Tower on Saturday. Whenever I think of the Tower, I think of you. I saw it from Formby Point last night. Just think it's almost two years to the day so we'll have to celebrate. What a marvellous two years they have been even though during the first we didn't see each other all that much. Hasn't this last year been great with all the places we've been and the laughs we've had. It's all been worth it because it was you. Anyway, I want to have lots and lots more years with you, all my years, in fact.

They're getting at me to switch off the light so I'll stop writing now. I'll have to get up early and finish my work.

I _do_ love you, L xxxx

P.S. Paul seems to like walking round the van in the nude. Is he kinky? Who knows? One consolation is that his bed is farthest from mine and I have Bernie if I need protection.

Lots of love, L xxxx

*October 1967*

Dear M,

You were right when you said that I really didn't know how much you loved me when we were at Southport Bus Station. When we were talking seriously about us, I got carried away and started trying to analyse things too deeply. I never want us to finish and I don't feel obligated to you. I do in some ways feel responsible for you because I love you. When I'm with you I'm as happy as I ever thought I could be. I meant it when I said that I could spend the rest of my life with you.

I hope all this worrying isn't affecting you at home or at school. I want us to have lots more great times together in the future. I love you, I really do. You know how I sometimes say things without realising the effects. Please write and tell me you love me. I can't bear knowing that you're unhappy.

I love you, L xxxxxx

October 1967

Dear M,

I've just got back to the van. I've been sitting on that marker thing on the beach for ages, about two hours, I think. I've been thinking and having a bit of a weep. I've come to the conclusion that I would write you a convincing letter saying exactly how I feel to prove to you how much I really love you. Then I wondered what on earth I could say to prove it to you. In science you can prove things by tests but I don't think there's a test to prove love.

You know I'm not always good at clearly explaining my feelings. I know I said that I _thought_ I loved you but had nothing to compare you with. That's probably all to do with me being a scientist. Everything has to be 100% before it is totally accepted. Anyway, after my long think I realised I don't _think_ I love you nor do I think I _must_ love you but I'm _absolutely sure_ I love you. The only thing is will you believe me? It must be difficult for you after what I said. Please tell me you believe me and love me. Please, please don't say you'll finish with me. I don't know what I'd do without you if you did. I couldn't bear it. I know how upset you were and I'm so sorry for hurting you. You know I don't always express myself very well when talking about feelings. If you really can't forgive me, please say so but don't leave me hanging on. I'm so sorry about what I said. All the marvellous things we've done and places we've been must mean as much to you as they do to me so please try to forgive me.

In one of the last films we saw, I think it was John Mills who said, 'Life's peculiar. Sometimes it makes you laugh and other times it makes you bloody cry.' Well, at the moment that's all I can do.

I love you so much, L xxxxx

P.S. Please, please believe me.

October 1967

Dear M,

Your letter was at the Union this morning and it really cheered me up. I'm so glad everything is all right between us again. I really hate seeing you unhappy. We have been through so much together and still have such a lot to look forward to. You know how much I love you and I always will.

I didn't have to do the long trek back to the van as Bernie was flashing past at the station just as I came out so it saved me a walk. He has started up again with Liz, half-started with Jackie and packed up Linda. I think he could write a book but our story would be much, much better. I'm sure that we would never tire of each other as we share and enjoy so many different things. In the future there will be lots more we can do together when we have more money and time.

Did you watch that film on TV about the runner who was a Borstal boy. I thought Tom Courtenay was really good as Smith. I think I'll have to get the book sometime.

I have decided that this week will be a work week. It's about time I did some. I had a tutorial this afternoon and it was awful. Nobody knew anything but Ken managed to save the day when he talked about his industrial experience this summer.

Don't forget to put your watch back. An extra hour in bed - wish we could share it together.

Hope you have a good week at school and if the brats misbehave give them an extra punishment from me.

All my love, L xxxxxxx

P.S. I'll try to dream about you.

November 1967

Dear M,

Here I am again, the perfect example of the clean living, immaculately groomed, intelligent and keen British undergraduate - and how! I haven't shaved since Sunday, my shoes need cleaning and my shirt has Guiness stains down the front. Do you think I'm like everyone imagines a typical student or am I not quite up, or rather down, to their ideas of what a student is like?

Anyway, enough of that. I'm quite happy at the moment. I've been thinking quietly about you and all the fantastic things we get up to. It's not the same being here without you while you are on TP but it's now nearly halfway through the term and next year will soon come. I can't wait. 3:30 has just struck. I wonder if you are still teaching now. I wish I was there with you or even being taught by you. I bet they buy you a present when TP is over. Drop the hint that you would like some bubbly and we'll have it for Christmas. Don't forget, the champers will really flow on our 21sts. I just think we should go out and shock everyone by getting married. That would be a laugh wouldn't it? There's an implication there that I'd be willing to spend all my life with you and want to more than anything.

I saw a couple of chaps I know vaguely today and they asked me how you were and they said how nice you seemed so in a way it made me feel quite proud.

I love you.

L xxxxx

P.S. How about changing your name to Mauretchka? - Sounds good. It means 'my darling little M'.

Your ever loving, gorgeous, sweet, handsome, virile, manly, suave but oh too modest, L xxxxx

November 1967

Dear M,

Well here I am doing yet another action-packed, scintillating metallurgy practical. There's nothing quite like cooking metal! It's a full day today with three lectures and this practical so I'll be ready for a rest tonight.

Yesterday I read some of that Albert Camus book on the train. It's quite good. I have tried a bit of the other one by de Beauvoir, but I found it really hard going.

Last night we decided to do some training for the match on Wednesday against Social Sciences. We put our gear on and ran about three miles in dense fog. We got lots of strange looks. I suppose it must have been a bit odd seeing three panting chaps in shorts in the middle of a damp, foggy night in November.

There's a Met Soc do a week on Saturday at Wyncote. It's a cheese and wine party. It should be good as all the crowd will be there. Could you come? If the last one is anything to go by it should be all right. There's no group but there'll be records and dancing, anyway please try to come. You could put your hair up. I hope you do 'cause you look ever so nice with it like that.

*I'm dying to see you at weekend. You'd better bring your boots as it takes just under half an hour from the station to the van. B is going home on Friday afternoon and P is going to Manchester to see his girlfriend. The only trouble will be getting to the toilet. It's all right for certain things but it could get a bit cold doing the other.*

*It seems ages since I've seen you so can't wait for weekend.*

*Love you lots, L xxxxxx*

*P.S. You'd better bring some warm clothes and a raincoat as well as the boots.*

November 1967

Dear M,

At the moment I am halfway through cooking yet more metal. Should be finished around 4:30 if I'm lucky.

We went to the nearest pub to the station last night. It was warm and pleasant. Then we went to Southport _as_ it's nearer to Formby than the Union by about six miles. We went in that pub where we went that fantastic afternoon we had at Ainsdale.

This will be the last letter you get before Friday so please write by return and tell me what time you're coming so I can meet you at the station. I'll have to get some food in so if there's anything special that you want just let me know. I'll get a couple of Vesta packets and some beer anyway.

Hope your throat's better. My headaches haven't been helped much by banging my head on the top of the van last night. Bernie thinks that someone has been trying to break in as there were some new scratch marks on the paintwork round the door. It wouldn't have been a very fruitful attempt unless they were after science notes or dirty laundry.

When we got back to the van the other day it was like a sandstorm. The sandhills surrounding the site looked as if they were on fire. There was so much sand flying around like thick smoke. It was awful going out to the toilet.

It will be great being able to be together for a whole weekend. I'm dying to see you as I've missed you a lot. I wish I could see you _every_ day.

I love you, L xxxxxxx

November 1967

Dear M,

What do I love in Liverpool?

The Phil
You
The Ferries
You
The Everyman
You
The Red Pearl Chinese
You
The Pier Head hotdogs
You

Most of all I love YOU. L xxxxx

November 1967

Dear M,

How are you? I've been thinking about you and feeling just a little bit lustful. I was thinking about those long, hot, steamy baths we had with you leaning back on me and my arms around you. We'll have to resume them next term when you're back at college. I've really missed our weekends together in Kirkby.

I've just had an hour on a microscope, testing and measuring holes in a bit of metal. It works using green and red lights so everything I see is green. I think it makes me a bit squint-eyed so if I look funny next time you see me that's why.

We've all been trying to work but with little success. This morning, maths was so boring that Bernie and I were drawing cartoons instead of taking notes. We were also sending messages to each other on bits of paper. It's a bit childish I suppose but it was really dreary.

A change of digs is on the cards after Christmas. Speaking of cards have you any left over from those you purloined last summer? We are moving back into Liverpool and will be back to civilisation after a term in the caravan. I'm not sure of the address yet but I'll let you know.

I had better finish as I don't want to miss the train.

Thinking of you.

I love you. L xxxxxxxx

P.S. Don't cane too many brats.

December 1967

Dear M,

Thanks for the great letter which I received this morning. I hope you got mine.

We played football this afternoon and won for a change, 2-1. I slipped and cut my knee and it's still bleeding a bit but I'll live.

Not much else has happened lately. We've all had good intentions of getting down to work but even though the spirit is willing, the flesh is weak, if that's the right way round.

Are you glad to have finished school? I am looking forward to next term when you are back in Kirkby. I've missed our weekends there so much. It will be great to just laze around together and do what we want without anyone else being there.

I'm afraid I'm not very inspired at the moment but pretty shattered after the match. Perhaps I need an early night to recover.

A funny thing keeps happening to me these days. When we're all together in the coffee bar or bar proper I keep going into a sort of trance and people have to jog me to get me out of it. I know what it is though. It's when I'm thinking of you and wishing I could be with you. Anyway, next term will come quite quickly. I can't wait.

The other day I heard **The Leaving of Liverpool** on the radio. I always think of you when I hear it. I sort of think of it as our tune. 'So fare thee well my own true love. When I return united we will be. It's not the leaving of Liverpool that grieves me but my darling when I think of thee'.

As ever, all my love, L xxxxxx

P.S. Luv the bones of ya, queen xxxxxx

December 1967

Dear M,

I love you. I love you. Oh, I really do! I don't know what I'd do without you - you are everything to me. I can't imagine any purpose in life other than living to be with you.

Last night on the train and tonight I could only think of you. I do love you. Just being next to you makes me feel great. The thought that I make you happy makes me feel like the king of the world. I just wish you could be with just me, by ourselves, completely alone all the time.

I reckon we would have a simply fantastic time together. We know so much about each other and seem so suited to each other that I think we would hit it off, so to speak, under the most adverse conditions. Please let's live together when we're finished with college.

I love you. I love you. I love you. I really hope you can read my writing as I am rather tipsy.

Isn't just sleeping together and lying with each other in bed simply great? When we are together like that it seems to be the whole purpose of life, just doing whatever we like whenever we like without any thought for anyone else except the person you think the world of - and I think the world of you. Please come and see me tomorrow.

Do you remember when we first knew each other and we didn't believe in love? It has really changed and I've no regrets.

I keep thinking of us living together or even being married and with the money coming in, what a marvellous time we could have together. I wish we were together this instant, just me and you. We really love each other and to me that's all that counts.

Love you always, L xxxxxx

December 1967

Dear M,

My ma doesn't seem to mind me coming over next week. I think my dad does but he's not been too bad - it must be the Christmas spirit or something.

Any idea what we're going to do at Christmas? If there's nothing special, I suppose we could go to the Stanley or the Jazz Club. We always have a good night up there don't we? If the weather's not too bad we could always take Shandy for a few walks.

I mentioned to my ma that I was considering working in France next summer and she said it was a good idea mainly because I wouldn't be at home with my dad like he is. It would be great if we could get a job together in France somewhere. I wouldn't mind what it was as long as we're together as long as possible instead of odd nights and days. I'm looking forward to when we can spend _our own_ Christmas together. All we would need would be a Woolies two and six tree with a bit of tinsel, a selection of booze and a big, warm, comfy bed. I can't wait!

I can't afford to buy your ma and pa much of a Christmas present. I'll get them some Christmas-wrapped chocolates if that's all right. I haven't bought you anything yet so I might surprise you.

I gave my pint of blood on Wednesday. Some people were flaking out like ninepins, but I was all right of course - my virility and strength showing through yet again.

Looking forward to seeing you on the 23$^{rd}$.

I love you. L xxxxx

P.S. Thanks for the very ego-boosting opening to your last letter.

*January 1968*

*Dear M,*

*I've had a good day today, just one lecture. In the afternoon we were supposed to play a football match but the other team never turned up so we gained a moral victory. We had a kick around instead and now I'm absolutely knackered but don't worry I shall be fully recovered by weekend.*

*This evening we went to a lecture on hypnotism. It was really interesting. I never believed in it before but I do now. I didn't volunteer. Anyway I'll tell you all about it at weekend. After that we had a pint in the Union bar and had fish and chips down West Derby Road on the way back to the digs.*

*Bernie bought a guitar yesterday so until he's learnt how to play it properly, I don't suppose we'll get much quiet or sleep. He keeps repeating the same G and C chords which is really annoying. I don't think Jimi Hendrix needs to worry.*

*When we were in the Union bar we saw some contestants for the Panto Queen contest and you were better than all of them so you should be Panto Queen and I'll be Panto King.*

*I love you. L xxxxxxx*

February 1968

Dear M,

It was nice to talk to you even if we didn't get much time. It's funny how we sometimes get cut off - I suppose it's when the money doesn't catch and the pips don't work either.

I think you must have got the days mixed up a bit because 21 days from that Monday is next Monday so you're not due for a few days yet. Still from previous experience you should be fine. I do worry though, as always, but let's not be too pessimistic.

Do you think my writing is awful? I was told off about it the last time I handed in a practical. Still, so long as you can read it, everything's fine.

Today I was wondering what to do when I've finished in Liverpool, or when Liverpool has finished with me, as the case may be. Management appeals to me but I don't seem to fit the dynamic, young executive type with the trendy, red sports car. To be quite honest I haven't got a clue what to do. Perhaps I should try training college. Teaching does seem a good idea, maybe not as cushy as it seems, but think of all the holiday time we could spend together - maybe not as I don't think I would survive another year in a training situation.

I hope the joke is worth hearing. I've got three to tell you. One in exchange for three isn't too bad is it?

Anyway, keep up your economy drive. I should probably help you by having one myself as long as it doesn't stop us having a good time.

Love you forever, L xxxxx

March 1968

Dear M,

It seems strange at the moment. I haven't seen you since last Sunday and I really wish you were here with me now. You know I will always love you no matter what.

The factory visits are still going on. Some are more boring than others. The one this morning was quite interesting. It showed us the fabrication of ships' propellors. You probably think that sounds very dreary but it was OK.

Tonight I went to a pub in town where the metallurgists tend to congregate. I had a pint with one of the lecturers. We had a good conversation and he seemed quite human away from the lecture room and labs.

At the moment, I don't feel like going home for Easter. I'd rather spend the time with you. That would be nice. Even if we do have a baby together it will make absolutely no difference to the way I feel about you. I just hope and pray that it will make no difference to the way you feel about me. My life would be empty without you.

I keep wishing that just the two of us could be together all the time without any interference from our parents or anyone. Let's buy that remote island with Fingal's Cave on it. We could take it over and build a little house there and call ourselves the Anglo, Irish, Polish Family. Anyway, I'm certain our day will come one day and for me it really is worth waiting for. I hope you feel the same. You know I won't desert you no matter what. I love you too much.

Love you forever, L xxxxxxx

March 1968

Dear M,

I have just completed a day's factory visits and it's been Harvey's 21st birthday. The factory visits were extremely boring but Harvey's party was great. His dad owns an off licence and he gave us two eight-pint cans of beer, 48 bottles of Newcastle Brown and two crates of Guinness. It was great and I wish you'd been there.

We're on our way to Warrington at the moment which accounts for my scrawly writing due to the bumping and lurching of the coach. My head is thumping as I haven't really sobered up properly after last night. I don't think I've ever been as drunk.

I'll come and see you on Saturday to please both you and Shandy. I am really missing you. It seems strange not to be able to talk on the phone and I miss that. I'm looking forward to the time we shall be able to talk to each other all the time.

I am now back at the digs. The visits were awful. I would have found more interest in a clothes peg. I don't think I properly sobered up until late afternoon and now the thought of Mrs G's tea is almost making me feel sick.

I'm glad you managed to get the job at Woolies. I'll finish now to catch the post. Love you always. Like the song says, 'There's no living without your loving'.

All my love, L xxxxxxxx

April 1968

Dear M,

How are you? I'm in bed now recovering after a hard day's visits. It really is hard tramping around factories. I hope your job is going all right. I suppose by now you are sick of the sight of Easter eggs. You'll have to save me one of those little, gooey ones.

It seemed strange being in tonight because I think we have been out together nearly every Wednesday this term. So it will be extra nice when I do eventually see you on Saturday. How are things at home? I wonder if you wish that you were here in Liverpool. Sometimes I wish we didn't have holidays then it would be so much easier for us to see each other whenever we want to.

We played a very energetic game of football in the garden of the digs tonight with the landlady's sons (aged 9 and 11). Bernie and I beat them convincingly 21-9 and 10-9 in two exciting games.

I've just started to pack my bags so here's hoping they won't take three weeks to get there. If they do, it will then be time to come back. I got a letter from Blackpool corporation today. Apparently all the jobs for students on the buses and trams have already been taken so I'll have to think of something else to see me over the summer.

Another poster has just fallen off the ceiling so now only three are remaining. It must be the fine weather I suppose. Have you seen Caroline lately? It must be a horrible experience for her to go through.

Is Shandy still missing me? I suppose she must be. If I can't sleep with you the next best thing is sleeping with Shandy if you see what I mean. She's lovely and cuddly too!

All this getting up early is going to be the end of me. Mind you, on Friday we are getting a meal on board on of the firm's newest ships which is supposed to be really good so that's something to look forward to.

I'll read for a while before I finally drop off to sleep. I might literally drop off the bed since the books I used to support the bed are in my case now.

Dying to see you on Saturday.

I love you. L xxxxxxxxx

*April 1968*

*Tonight when my dad came home from work there was an awful row because I didn't come back on Sunday. The trouble is if I'm going to have any peace at home I had better not come and stay at your place these holidays. I'm so sorry about this and I feel like I've let you down.*

*Please come on the coach on Saturday night to see me - please. I feel really miserable at the moment. Try to forgive me. We'll soon be back in Liverpool and everything will be all right.*

*I hope you've had a better day than me. I'm sorry but at the moment I'm so depressed I can't write any more.*

*I'll love you always, L*

*xxxxx xxxxx xxxxx*

*April 1968*

*Dear M,*

I <u>AM</u> *coming on Friday because I think it's worth it just for one day. If you say it isn't worth it you may as well say that all the times we met during the week last term were not worth it because then we were together for much less time than we will be on Friday. Of course it's worth it! Surely it's better than not seeing each other at all.*

*From what you said it seems like you don't want me to come at all, probably because of what I said about my row with my dad. It's hopeless trying to argue rationally with him. Whenever we argue, all he says is that I'm too big-headed since I went to university. He's not just said this about university but about passing A-levels, being in the sixth form, passing O-levels, being in the express form, going to grammar school, even getting a motorbike and on any occasion when I have achieved something. He says things like I'm too big for my boots and I put myself above everyone else and that's his usual argument. I've told him what I think of him but it only makes him shout louder. He said that if I stayed overnight at your place he would come and drag me home and kick* up a hell of a fuss in the process. He would too. He dragged me away from a party once when I was 16 when I went and tried to call his bluff so I'm certain he would do it again. Just think of all the trouble it would cause if he did come. Not staying this holiday is a sort of precaution.

He also practically threw me out of the house. I would have gone but I had no money and it was my ma that saved me from actually doing it and tried to calm him down.

It seems that when you have a row at your house everything returns to normal after a while but that doesn't happen here with my dad. He just constantly holds every single thing against me. He's got so much against me it's unbelievable. If it happens again, I shall leave home as it's the best thing to do. Sometimes I just hate him and his grudges. This summer I think I will try to get a flat somewhere to avoid going home to Blackpool. It's probably for the best.

I'm really sorry about all this but if you love me as you say you do then we'll soon get over this - probably the instant we both set foot in Liverpool again.

This morning I was lying in bed thinking about you and all the ridiculous and fantastic things we have done over the last couple of years and all the things we might do in the future. We are not going to let this upset spoil everything between us because it is so insignificant compared to all the happy times we have had and will have - if you still want me that is.

I love you as always. L xxxxxxxx

P.S. I can't bear not seeing you so I will be there on Friday xxxxxx

*May 1968*

*Dear M,*

*Whichever way you look at it...*

It it IT **IT**

IT it IT *it* 𝒥𝒯

It **IT** it

*I LOVE YOU XXXXXXXXXX*

July 1968

Dear M,

I wrote a letter on Sunday morning before I went to work and posted it on the way there. As I haven't heard from you I wondered if you received it. It's funny but when I was working before it seemed worth it, but now I don't see you very much because of the long hours and limited free time, it doesn't. It used to be great finishing college or work then dashing off to see you. When I wake up on Saturday, knowing I'll be seeing you soon, it will make life worth living again.

Do you remember the first time we went to the Isle of Man and I said that I wanted to get engaged, well it was from that point I knew I wanted to marry you. Somehow it seemed to me that being engaged would be a tighter bond but now I realise I didn't need that extra assurance. Since that time all that has had any importance to me is being with you and knowing that we love each other. I can't wait for Saturday night.

Please write me one of those special letters. I love you so much.

All my love always, L xxxxxxxxx

August 1968

Dear M,

It's always horrible when we part but soon we won't have to part, like on Saturday, anymore. Sometimes I feel like the loneliest person in the world except when I am with you and then everything is wonderful. Even when we're just sitting on the settee watching TV, just touching you or putting my arms around you always makes me feel fine again.

There's no doubt that getting married is a very large step to take but with you I'm sure we will succeed because I can't see us changing in any way and my feelings for you will always be the same. The more I think about it the more I want us to be together always. When we are married no one can keep us apart.

While waiting for the bus at Preston bus station, a drunk man sat next to me. He put his hand on my knee and started chatting in an overly-friendly way. I said that my wife would soon be back with a cup of tea... He then got up and lurched away. It felt good to say 'my wife'.

Next Saturday will soon come and we can go to the Scotch Bar if you feel up to it. If you don't, we can have a meal or go to the pictures.

I was thinking that soon the Stanley Arms will be my local pub which quite appeals to me. We can take Shandy for walks then call in for some refreshments. It will be great. See you on Saturday.

Love you forever.

L xxxxxxxxx

September 1968

Dear M,

I was back in time for work. My dad didn't say anything, just gave me strange looks.

I finished work at midnight on Sunday. There wasn't much to do because many of the shops would be closed for the bank holiday. We got another new chap on the line. I don't know how long he will last. He looked quite ill when he saw us bashing hot Slimcea rolls out of the tins. I slept right through until two o'clock this afternoon and I still feel tired. It's been hard work and I'll be glad to finally finish, although the money is good and I've saved quite a bit. I'll have to find something that pays well when we are married.

It was great at the Stanley on Saturday night. I've not seen you so cheerful for ages. It was fabulous when you came down during the night and we held each other close. Just think, in less than a fortnight we will be married and be able to sleep together every night without anyone objecting. It will probably take a bit of the devilment away, but none of the pleasure and excitement.

I love you. L xxxxxx

P.S. You aren't one of those 'gold-diggers', just marrying me for my money are you?

All my love xxxxxx

On the 14<sup>th</sup> September 1968,
at the local registry office, he said to her,
'Will you marry me?'

She said to him, 'I will.'

They did!

Milton Keynes UK
Ingram Content Group UK Ltd.
UKHW040956140324
439439UK00001B/193

9 781803 814148